SPECTRUM®

Vocabulary

Grade 6

Published by Spectrum®
an imprint of Carson-Dellosa Publishing LLC
Greensboro, NC

Spectrum®
An imprint of Carson-Dellosa Publishing LLC
P.O. Box 35665
Greensboro, NC 27425 USA

ISBN 0-7696-8086-0

07-090127784

Table of Contents

Skills Practice

Classification 4
Synonyms 10
Antonyms 15
Homonyms 20
Context Clues 26
Concept Words 32
Sensory Words 38
Plurals 43
Suffixes 47
Prefixes 53
Root and Base Words 59
Imported Words 67
Abbreviations 73
Compound Words 77
Vocabulary Answer Key 83

Test-taking Practice

Introduction to Test-taking Practice 103
Test-taking Tips 104
Test-taking in Vocabulary 106
Test-taking in Reading Comprehension 120
Test-taking Practice Answer Key 149
Test-taking Student Answer Sheet 153

Name _____

Classification means to put words together in **groups**. A word **analogy** expresses the **relationship between words**. Complete each analogy with an appropriate word.

1. Cup is to adult as bottle is to _____

2. Four is to dog as two is to _____

3. Skin is to human as feathers are to _____

4. Paw is to dog as hoof is to _____

5. Hot is to oven as cold is to _____

6. Watch is to wrist as ring is to _____

7. Round is to ball as square is to _____

8. Calf is to cow as foal is to _____

9. Antlers are to deer as horns are to _____

10. Ink is to pen as paint is to _____

11. Rain is to spring as snow is to _____

12. Tadpole is to frog as caterpillar is to _____

Name _____

Two of the most common analogies involve synonyms and antonyms.

Model 1:   *Word* is to *word* as *word* is to _____.
                      (synonym)   (synonym)
Example: *Small* is to *little* as *big* is to *large*.

Model 2:   *Word* is to *word* as *word* is to _____.
                      (antonym)   (antonym)
Example: *Beautiful* is to *ugly* as *happy* is to *sad*.

Read the definitions of the words in the word box. Complete the analogies below using words from the word box.

timid—*adj.* without courage   **jovial—*adj.*** full of laughter, jolly

sullen—*adj.* gloomy, bad humored   **climate—*n.*** weather conditions

foe—*n.* enemy   **loathe—*v.*** to dislike, to detest

bold—*adj.* showing great courage   **comprehend—*v.*** to understand

1. *Bad* is to *terrible* as *shy* is to _____.

2. *Bad* is to *good* as _____ is to *friend*.

3. *Car* is to *automobile* as *weather* is to _____.

4. *Teach* is to *instruct* as *understand* is to _____.

5. *Shout* is to *whisper* as *love* is to _____.

6. *Mean* is to *kind* as *shy* is to _____.

7. *Gentle* is to *rough* as *happy* is to _____.

8. *Pretty* is to *cute* as _____ is to *jolly*.

9. *Love* is to *like* as _____ is to *detest*.

10. *Bush* is to *shrub* as *enemy* is to _____.

Read the analogy models, then circle the correct word to complete each analogy below. Use a dictionary if you need help.

Model 1: *Tool* is to its *function* as *tool* is to its _____.
(function)

Example: *Pen* is to *writing* as *shovel* is to *digging*.

Model 2: *Title* is to *specialty* as *title* is to _____.
(specialty)

Example: *Dentist* is to *teeth* as *veterinarian* is to *animals*.

Model 3: *Cause* is to *effect* as *cause* is to _____.
(effect)

Example: *Sadness* is to *tears* as *joy* is to *laughter*.

Model 4: *Worker* is to *product* as *worker* is to _____.
(product)

Example: *Author* is to *book* as *artist* is to *painting*.

1. *Policeman* is to *crime* as *doctor* is to _____.
   a. illness b. nurse c. stethoscope d. patient
2. *Carpenter* is to *hammer* as *doctor* is to _____.
   a. illness b. nurse c. stethoscope d. patient
3. *Druggist* is to *pharmacy* as *teacher* is to _____.
   a. student b. school c. books d. teach
4. *Baker* is to *bread* as *seamstress* is to _____.
   a. thread b. needle c. dress d. sewing
5. *Scissors* are to *cut* as *ax* is to _____.
   a. chop b. burn c. tree d. sharpen
6. *Sun* is to *sunburn* as *snow* is to _____.
   a. overcast b. frostbite c. umbrella d. climate
7. *Fire* is to *burn* as *cold* is to _____.
   a. ice b. freeze c. snow d. wind
8. *Hunger* is to *eat* as *thirst* is to _____.
   a. food b. cup c. milk d. drink

Name _____

Look up each of the following words in a dictionary and write the definitions on the line. Then, use these words to complete each analogy below.

 1. **punctual** _____

 2. **fragile** _____

 3. **discard** _____

 4. **fraudulent** _____

 5. **peril** _____

 6. **prohibit** _____

 7. **monotonous** _____

 8. **decade** _____

 9. **augment** _____

10. **soothe** _____

11. *Food* is to *eat* as *trash* is to _____.

12. *Late* is to *early* as *tardy* is to _____.

13. *Metal* is to *sturdy* as *glass* is to _____.

14. *Accept* is to *reject* as *allow* is to _____.

15. *Loud* is to *quiet* as *varied* is to _____.

16. *Real* is to *genuine* as *fake* is to _____.

17. *One hundred* is to *century* as *ten* is to _____.

18. *Hard* is to *soft* as *disturb* is to _____.

19. *Take* is to *give* as *subtract* is to _____.

20. *Walk* is to *stroll* as *danger* is to _____.

Name _____

MAKE NO BONES
ABOUT IT!
SCIENCE IS FUN!

Classify each animal from the word box. Write it in the correct column.

Vertebrates (backbones)	**Invertebrates** (no backbones)
1. _____	1. _____
2. _____	2. _____
3. _____	3. _____
4. _____	4. _____
5. _____	5. _____
6. _____	6. _____
7. _____	7. _____
8. _____	8. _____
9. _____	9. _____
10. _____	10. _____
11. _____	11. _____
12. _____	12. _____

starfish	horned toad	mosquito	gerbil
ostrich	praying mantis	blue whale	sponge
octopus	sting ray	aardvark	jellyfish
cicada	Great Dane	king snake	sailfish
moose	woodpecker	butterfly	warthog
snail	earthworm	glowworm	sand dollar

Name _____

Each word in Bank A shares a feature with a word in Bank B. Place each word with its appropriate feature. Then write another word which shares this feature.

Feature	Bank A word	Bank B word	Your Word
1. sense organ	ear	nose	eye
2. inventor			
3. fabric			
4. to be read			
5. city			
6. direction			
7. musical genre			
8. disease			
9. color			
10. in Washington, D.C.			
11. school subject			
12. body of water			
13. Shakespearean character			
14. communication tool			
15. South American country			

Bank A: Bolivia, chicken pox, cotton, Denver, Edison, fuchsia, newspaper, Nile River, north, rock, Romeo, Smithsonian, history, telephone

Bank B: Carver, Chesapeake Bay, Hamlet, jazz, Lincoln Memorial, magazine, Paraguay, polyester, English, Santa Fe, south, strep throat, telegraph, turquoise

Name _____

Write a word from the word box next to its synonym.

refuse	occur	shake	choose
purchase	fright	rough	reply
copy	vacant	worth	pledge
genuine	depart	simple	tardy

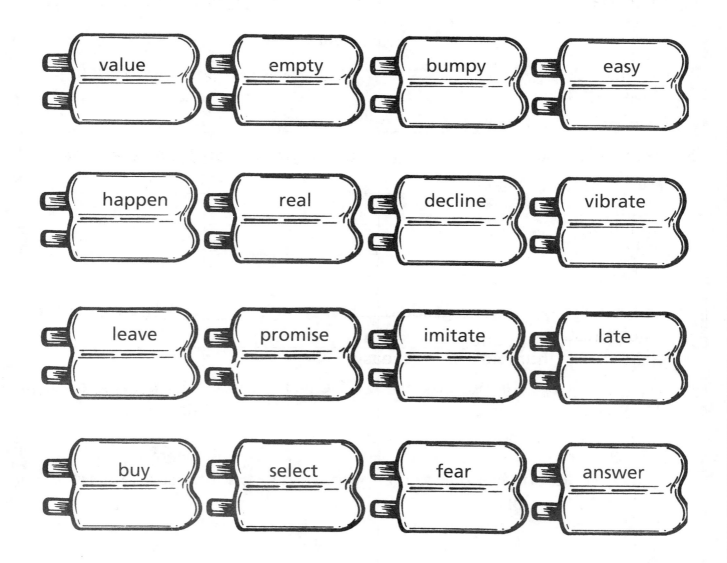

value

empty

bumpy

easy

happen

real

decline

vibrate

leave

promise

imitate

late

buy

select

fear

answer

Name _____

Read each sentence carefully. Write the word that best completes each sentence on the line.

1. When my friends gave me a surprise birthday party, I was so surprised that I was _____ (synonym for quiet).
   shy   **speechless**   **peaceful**

2. She was so _____ (synonym for quiet) that she couldn't speak in front of the class.
   shy   **speechless**   **peaceful**

3. We love going to the mountain cabin because it is so _____ (synonym for quiet) there.
   shy   **speechless**   **peaceful**

4. The meat was so _____ (synonym for hard) that I could barely chew it.
   tough   **difficult**   **firm**

5. The test was so _____ (synonym for hard) that everyone failed.
   tough   **difficult**   **firm**

6. I didn't sleep well because the mattress was too _____ (synonym for hard).
   tough   **difficult**   **firm**

7. He is sure to get a good grade on that _____ (synonym for simple) test.
   plain   **humble**   **easy**

8. The girl was wearing a very _____ (synonym for simple) blue dress.
   plain   **humble**   **easy**

9. The home of the poor farmer was quite _____ (synonym for simple).
   plain   **humble**   **easy**

Name _____

Circle the synonym of each highlighted word. Write each circled word on its numbered line to form a sentence. Use a dictionary to help you.

1. **wing**	arm	fly	feather	cable (3)
2. **oceans**	continents	lakes	vistas	seas (6)
3. **fowls**	pteranodons	rabbits	birds	bones (1)
4. **spacious**	vast	burgeon	absent	mouthful (5)
5. **beyond**	toward	against	past	near (4)
6. **noiselessly**	silently	surely	amusingly	slowly (2)

_____   _____   _____   _____   _____   _____
(1)   (2)   (3)   (4)   (5)   (6)

1. **ascended**	mastered	shuffled	climbed	twisted (4)
2. **compliant**	taciturn	shy	obsolete	obedient (2)
3. **ancient**	hardened	transient	absolute	old (6)
4. **warily**	merely	cautiously	extreme	tiredly (1)
5. **grating**	creaky	charming	boxing	stony (5)
6. **benches**	stiles	spines	goals	pews (7)
7. **juveniles**	renegades	children	parrots	villains (3)

_____   _____   _____   _____   _____   _____   _____
(1)   (2)   (3)   (4)   (5)   (6)   (7)

1. **brawny**	dour	clean	stout	smart (2)
2. **determinedly**	thoughtfully	sanely	resolutely	mutely (7)
3. **toted**	hauled	gave	wrote	painted (4)
4. **cases**	shelves	levers	tops	cartons (6)
5. **roustabouts**	angels	chickens	grievances	laborers (3)
6. **a gross**	20	money	short	144 (1)
7. **icebox**	frigid	refrigerator	cubic	storage (5)

_____   _____   _____   _____   _____   _____   _____
(1)   (2)   (3)   (4)   (5)   (6)   (7)

Name _____

Write a word from the word box that has the same meaning.

pan	yell	house	glue	rip	bag
dish	gift	cry	sick	cup	smile

shout _____	plate _____
home _____	present _____
grin _____	weep _____
paste _____	tear _____
ill _____	mug _____
pot _____	sack _____

Name _____

Circle the pair of synonyms in each box. Complete each sentence with one of the circled words.

| noisy | quiet | loud | fast |

1. The horns were _____.
2. The crowd was _____.

| rough | coarse | soft | straight |

3. Sand paper is _____.
4. Cement is _____.

| right | left | wrong | incorrect |

5. Never drive the _____ way on a one way street.
6. I got an _____ answer on the test.

| laugh | smile | cry | giggle |

7. Your _____ is contagious.
8. I can't help but _____ when I hear it.

| fix | break | repair | own |

9. We will _____ the car.
10. I can't _____ my watch myself.

| neat | quick | messy | clean |

11. _____ up the kitchen.
12. Keep your room _____ .

Name _____

Antonyms are words that mean the **opposite.** Write the antonym for each word below.

1. near   _____

2. easy   _____

3. first   _____

4. high   _____

5. stand   _____

6. best   _____

7. boy   _____

8. left   _____

9. question   _____

10. north   _____

11. huge   _____

12. organized   _____

Name _____

Write the antonym for the <u>underlined</u> word in each sentence. Use the words from the word box.

tough	easy
peaceful	talkative
outgoing	difficult
flashy	soft
full	

1. I was <u>speechless</u> when I got up
   to give my speech.   _____

2. I felt <u>shy</u> as the new girl
   at the party.   _____

3. Our neighbor's dogs make the
   neighborhood so <u>noisy</u>.   _____

4. The over-cooked steak was <u>soft</u>. _____

5. Can you help me with
   these <u>easy</u> questions?   _____

6. My pillow is extra <u>firm</u>.   _____

7. That test was so <u>difficult</u>!   _____

8. The theater was <u>empty</u> for
   Friday's new release.   _____

9. That striped and polka-dotted shirt
   you're wearing sure is <u>plain</u>.   _____

Name _____

Circle an antonym for the <u>underlined</u> word in each sentence.

1. The bike is <u>broken</u>.   fixed   old   lost

2. Kim is the <u>tallest</u> girl.   oldest   shortest   cutest

3. That <u>boy</u> is nice.   kid   girl   person

4. Steve is very <u>happy</u>.   angry   funny   sad

5. Can Mark <u>work</u> today?   run   play   eat

6. Jump <u>over</u> the net.   under   beside   on

7. I <u>found</u> the door key.   forgot   lost   hid

8. It <u>started</u> on time.   played   showed   stopped

9. I have a <u>hard</u> bed.   big   soft   tiny

10. The movie is <u>short</u>.   long   funny   sad

11. I was <u>early</u> today.   home   lost   late

12. He drives too <u>fast</u>.   slow   hurry   far

Name _____

Write the matching antonym for each word.

innocent	present	interior	victory	doubt	rare
defense	increase	shallow	few	wild	plain
departure	minimum	excited	lazy	smooth	rude

 common _____

 fancy _____

 absent _____

 deep _____

 many _____

 maximum_____

 rough _____

 polite _____

 arrival _____

 ambitious_____

 decrease_____

 offense _____

 exterior _____

 defeat _____

 believe _____

 calm _____

 guilty _____

 tame _____

Name _____

Circle the pair of antonyms in each box. Complete each sentence with one of the circled words.

| sweet | quiet | noisy | fast |

1. The blowing horns were _____.
2. It was _____ in the library.

| rough | empty | smooth | straight |

3. The cat's fur felt _____.
4. The sandpaper was _____.

| close | wrong | near | right |

5. Never drive the _____ way on a one way street.
6. I got a prize for having the _____ answer.

| bought | decorated | sent | sold |

7. I _____ my bike when I outgrew it.
8. Mom _____ me a warmer jacket.

| laugh | sleepy | lose | find |

9. Did you _____ the key I lost?
10. In a strange place, it's easy to _____ your way.

| break | own | hurt | repair |

11. A flying ball might _____ a window.
12. He needed tools to _____ the car.

| worn | neat | messy | quick |

13. I had to clean my _____ desk.
14. I like my handwriting to look _____.

Name _____

Read these different meanings for the word **scale** and answer the questions.

1) thin plates on reptiles or fish
2) an object used to measure weight
3) to climb up the side
4) a map marking for distance
5) a group of musical notes

1. Which meaning of scale (1, 2, 3, 4, or 5) does each picture show?

○   ○   ○   ○   ○

2. Choose the correct meaning of **scale** in each sentence. Write the meaning on the line below the sentence.

A. The **scale** shows that the town is 15 miles away.

_____

B. Many dinosaurs had **scales**.

_____

C. I can play **scales** on the piano.

_____

D. She put the meat on a **scale**.

_____

E. He **scaled** the high mountain.

_____

Name _____

Read the list below.

sign	1) a symbol	2) to write your name
dash	1) a small amount	2) to run quickly
chief	1) leader	2) first or main
trip	1) journey	2) to stumble
quarter	1) one-fourth	2) 25 cent coin
company	1) visitor or guests	2) business

Decide which meaning the **boldfaced** word has in each sentence below. Fill in ① or ②. Then write the meaning on the line.

① ②   A. Be careful not to **trip** over the rock!

_____

① ②   B. We are having **company** tonight.

_____

① ②   C. When it started to rain, we made a **dash** for the house.

_____

① ②   D. They turned left at the stop **sign.**

_____

① ②   E. Mom gave me a **quarter** for my piggy bank.

_____

① ②   F. The **chief** of police spoke to us about safety.

_____

Name _____

Write the correct homonym in the matching room of the Homonym Hotel.

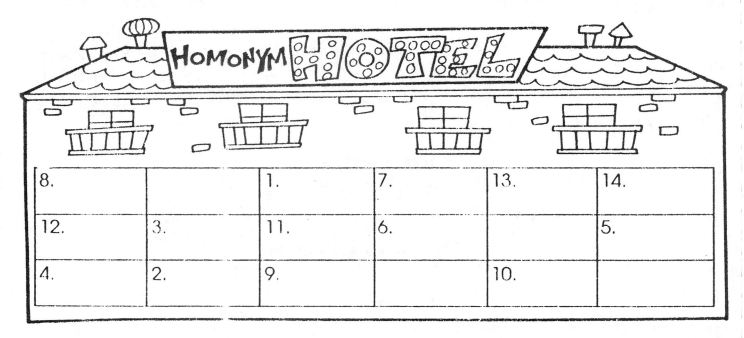

8.		1.	7.	13.	14.
12.	3.	11.	6.		5.
4.	2.	9.		10.	

1. The state of Nevada is mostly (desert, dessert).

2. The family went to Virginia (Beech, Beach).

3. The camper's letter began, (Dear, Deer) Mom and Dad.

4. They visited the (Capital, Capitol) building in Washington, D.C.

5. She (road, rode) the roller coaster four times!

6. (There, Their) minivan had a flat tire.

7. (Meet, Meat) me by the diving board at 3:00.

8. The prince sat on his royal (thrown, throne).

9. The elephants at the zoo (paste, paced) back and forth.

10. We (new, knew) our vacation would be in August.

11. Have you ever (bin, been) to New York City?

12. Our dinner was prepared in a Japanese (walk, wok).

13. Our (principle, principal) vacationed in Florida.

14. We toured an old English (manor, manner).

Name _____

Circle the homonyms that were misused in the story. Rewrite the story using the correct words.

Four to weaks, eye have Ben baking cakes with read icing. Ewe can knot waist flower and sugar, sew eye eight every won of the cakes. Of coarse, my waste is getting bigger. Eye am getting as big as a hoarse. The plane fact is, I blue my diet.

_____

_____

_____

_____

_____

_____

_____

_____

Name _____

Circle the homonyms that were misused in the story. Rewrite the story using the correct words.

Land of His Own

  The cowboy road his horse into town. He didn't waist any time getting there. He went to the bank to get a lone. He had to weight awhile. But soon he had money to by land of his own!

Land of His Own

_____

_____

_____

_____

_____

_____

Name _____

Circle each misused homonym and write the correct form on the lines below.

One mourning while weighting four the school bus, I felt a pane in my heal. It seams I had a whole inn my shoe and a peace of glass was cot inside.

1. _____

2. _____

3. _____

4. _____

5. _____

6. _____

7. _____

8. _____

9. _____

10. _____

Name _____

A **context clue** is a clue or **hint from the sentence** that helps you to figure out words that you don't know. Read each sentence carefully. Guess the definition of each <u>underlined</u> word based on the context clues in the sentence. Then use a dictionary to see how good your guess was.

1. He didn't want to miss that game because the coach had said it was a <u>crucial</u> one in deciding the championship.

   _____   _____
            your guess   dictionary definition

2. Although he tried to be <u>punctual,</u> he was always late.

   _____   _____
            your guess   dictionary definition

3. The confusing instructions that come with some home computers <u>perplex</u> many people.

   _____   _____
            your guess   dictionary definition

4. Light has a <u>velocity</u> of about 186,000 miles per second.

   _____   _____
            your guess   dictionary definition

5. Our pet bird <u>warbles</u> happily in his cage all day long.

   _____   _____
            your guess   dictionary definition

Name _____

Read each sentence. Guess the definition of the <u>underlined</u> word. Use a dictionary to check your guesses.

1. I get sunburned easily, so I <u>shun</u> long days at the beach.

_____   _____
       your guess   dictionary definition

2. He skied so well that no one could believe he was a <u>novice</u>.

_____   _____
       your guess   dictionary definition

3. We grew too many tomatoes, so we gave the <u>surplus</u> to the neighbors.

_____   _____
       your guess   dictionary definition

4. Our teacher <u>berated</u> us for being rude to the guest.

_____   _____
       your guess   dictionary definition

5. A promise of something for nothing is usually a <u>fraud</u>.

_____   _____
       your guess   dictionary definition

6. His <u>anguish</u> over his dog's death did not stop for many weeks.

_____   _____
       your guess   dictionary definition

7. If we want to stay on the team, we must <u>adhere</u> to the rules.

_____   _____
       your guess   dictionary definition

8. If our best hitter is ill, our chance of winning will <u>diminish</u>.

_____   _____
       Your guess   dictionary definition

Name _____

Read each sentence. Guess the definition of the <u>underlined</u> word. Use a dictionary to check your guesses.

1. You will get a ticket from the policeman if you <u>exceed</u> the speed limit.

   _____   _____
          your guess   dictionary definition

2. The park ranger asked us to <u>discard</u> our litter in the basket.

   _____   _____
          your guess   dictionary definition

3. Although he was in great <u>peril,</u> he risked his life to save the child.

   _____   _____
          your guess   dictionary definition

4. That is a <u>fragile</u> vase, so please handle it with care.

   _____   _____
          your guess   dictionary definition

5. He didn't go to the dentist because he feared <u>excruciating</u> pain.

   _____   _____
          your guess   dictionary definition

6. The rain made your note <u>illegible,</u> so we did not know where you had gone.

   _____   _____
          your guess   dictionary definition

7. She has purchased many new stamps to <u>augment</u> her collection.

   _____   _____
          your guess   dictionary definition

8. The <u>obstinate</u> mule refused to budge from the street.

   _____   _____
          your guess   dictionary definition

Name _____

Read each sentence. Guess the definition of the <u>underlined</u> word. Use a dictionary to check your guesses.

1. His <u>monotonous</u> speech made half the audience fall asleep.

   _____   _____
           your guess   dictionary definition

2. The fire department <u>prohibits</u> the use of candles in this theatre because of the fire danger.

   _____   _____
           your guess   dictionary definition

3. Her <u>cordial</u> welcome made all her guests feel at home.

   _____   _____
           your guess   dictionary definition

4. After the long hike, we all suffered from <u>fatigue</u>.

   _____   _____
           your guess   dictionary definition

5. The elephant looked <u>enormous</u> to the small boy.

   _____   _____
           your guess   dictionary definition

6. The snow <u>glistened</u> like jewels in the moonlight.

   _____   _____
           your guess   dictionary definition

7. Yesterday was a very <u>hectic</u> day because our relatives arrived from Alaska and the dog had puppies on the couch.

   _____   _____
           your guess   dictionary definition

8. When the man lost all his money, he became a <u>pauper</u>.

   _____   _____
           your guess   dictionary definition

Name _____

For each sentence, circle the pair of words that completes the meaning of the sentence.

1. Their profits have been _____, and they wish to _____ their situation.
   a. decreasing—excuse
   b. declining—remedy
   c. comfortable—redress

2. Rats provide a _____ in reducing garbage, but this is outweighed by their _____ activities.
   a. help—useful
   b. trouble—dynamic
   c. service—harmful

3. Fact and Fancy were so _____ that no one could _____ them.
   a. connected—separate
   b. necessary—use
   c. respected—want

4. If one is to understand the _____, one must study the _____.
   a. facts—unnecessary
   b. unusual—sentences
   c. whole—parts

5. His father _____ him, for he realized the interest was more than a _____ fancy.
   a. encouraged—childish
   b. berated—sincere
   c. helped—mature

6. Safe driving prevents _____ and the awful _____ of knowing you have caused an accident.
   a. disease—remainder
   b. accidents—safe
   c. tragedy—remorse

Name _____

Circle the word which best fits each sentence.

Saving your (1) _____ to eat at a later date is not always (2) _____.
It may not wait as long as you do!
1. land   greed   luck   dessert
2. golden   wise   fair   sure

Many (3) _____ may indeed make for light work, but only if they work
(4) _____.
3. shovels   seas   hands   kitchens
4. together   alone   nearby   silently

"Put your money where your mouth is" may be a (5) _____-inflicting
proverb; but it sure (6) _____ people quiet!
5. plant   gold   wise   germ
6. invests   keeps   shuts   tempts

Go ahead and rollerblade along life's (7) _____, but keep those knee
pads (8) _____ for the bumps along the way.
7. problems   lanes   lamps   deeds
8. ready   quick   dangerous   softly

Music may indeed (9) _____ a savage beast, but only if the (10)
_____ has an instrument nearby.
9. shoot   ride   calm   scale
10. lion   trumpet   radio   musician

The saying "A fool and his money are soon (11) _____" should not be
discussed when (12) _____ allowance off our folks.
11. parted   happy   peaceful   shown
12. sewing   waving   giving   begging

As Uncle Gene (13) _____ on his inflatable raft on the (14) _____,
we knew that some men are islands!
13. flew   fetched   floated   fared
14. dock   lake   sink   house

Hurtling downward into a deep, dark (15) _____, Bernard exclaimed,
"Why sure! Gotta (16) _____ before ya' leap!"
15. mansion   Chevy   chasm   rim
16. look   shave   care   buy

Name _____

Concept words are words that have to do with a certain **topic or subject.** Read the passage carefully.

Volcanoes!

Volcanoes are special kinds of mountains. Under volcanoes, deep in the earth, is a layer of hot, liquid rock called **magma**. Volcanoes are formed when the magma is suddenly forced up through a crack in the **crust**, or surface, of the earth. This action, called **eruption**, spills the hot magma, or lava, out onto the crust. As it cools, it hardens and forms mounds.

Scientists classify volcanoes in three groups. The first group includes volcanoes that have not erupted in hundreds of years. These volcanoes are **extinct** and are unlikely to erupt again. The second group also includes volcanoes that have not erupted in many years but these volcanoes are thought to be capable of erupting again. These volcanoes are called **dormant**. The final group includes volcanoes that erupted not long ago and could erupt again at any time. These volcanoes are said to be **active**.

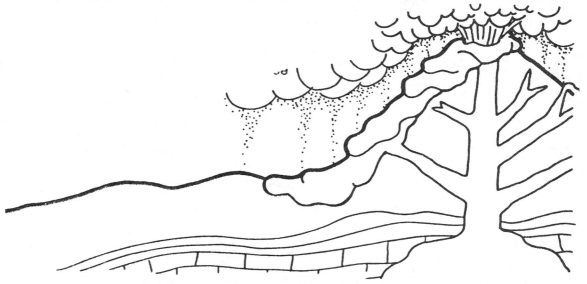

Find and write a **boldfaced** word from the story for each description.

1. _____ liquid rock beneath the earth

2. _____ group of volcanoes unlikely to erupt

3. _____ the outer surface of the earth

4. _____ action that forces magma through the crust

5. _____ group of volcanoes that have recently erupted

6. _____ group of volcanoes that have not erupted in many years but still may erupt

Name _____

Fill in the blanks to show the scientific process of respiration.

water	work	carbon dioxide
energy	sugar	oxygen
cells	roots	

Plant cells take in _____ and _____.

Tubes carry these from the leaves to the _____ and other

parts of the plant. The other plant parts use the carbon dioxide to break the

sugar down into _____ and _____ which

release _____. The _____ will use this

energy to do _____.

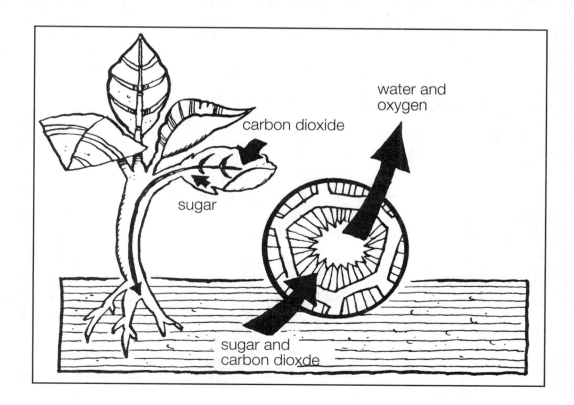

Name _____

Use the clues to complete the crossword puzzle on page 35.

Across

4. a substance that is formed when two elements chemically combine

5. a system that changes food into a form that cells can use

7. the force that pulls heavenly bodies toward each other

8. to use something over again

10. the force that resists motion between two objects in contact

11. a system that consists of the brain, spinal cord, and nerve fibers

12. a large muscle that helps you breathe

Down

1. an eclipse in which the moon moves through Earth's shadow

2. an eclipse in which the moon's shadow falls upon the Earth

3. a system that brings air into and out of the body

6. the shape of all the planets' orbits around the sun

9. two or more substances that are mixed together but not chemically combined

nervous system	friction	recycle
compound	diaphragm	gravity
digestive system	solar eclipse	mixture
respiratory system	lunar eclipse	ellipse

Name _____

CROSSWORD PUZZLES
BUILD BRAINPOWER!

Name _____

Read the passage carefully. Use each of the **boldfaced** words in a sentence below.

Hundreds of years ago, people believed in a **variety** of **mythical**, or imaginary, creatures. Two **legendary** characters from myths were the unnatural, strange-looking, grotesque creatures called **gargoyles**, and the **Cyclops**, a giant with one eye.

One of the most **attractive**, or likable, of mythical beasts was the sleek, one-horned, **unicorn**. Another famous animal was the flying horse, **Pegasus**. He had wings that carried him high into the sky.

Have you read about any of these **fantastic**, or strange, creatures?

1. The _____ characters came from myths or legends passed down through hundreds of years.

2. Grotesque, unnatural figures were known as _____.

3. _____ was a famous winged horse.

4. A mythical giant with one eye in the middle of its forehead was known as _____.

5. A _____ creature isn't real. It's imaginary.

6. A number of different kinds of things are a _____.

7. The unicorn, an _____ animal, was pleasing and likable.

8. The old, wild, or strange creatures seem _____ to us.

9. The _____, a mythical beast with one horn, is my favorite.

Name _____

Read the passage carefully.

Computer Data

Computers may seem "smart" but they cannot think. The only thing they can do is follow a set of instructions called a **program** which must be written by a person. The computer **hardware** (machinery) and **software** (programs) work together.

For the computer to work, a person must enter **data**, or information, into the computer. This is called **input**. New data is entered by typing on a **keyboard** that has letters and symbols like a typewriter. Data may be stored on a **disk** which is used to record and save information.

Next, the computer "reads" the data and follows the instructions of the program. The program may tell it to organize the data, compare it to other data, or store it for later use. This is called data **processing**.

When the processing is complete, the computer can display the results either on the screen or printed on paper as a **printout**.

Find and write a **boldfaced** word from the passage for each description.

1. _____ used to save and record information

2. _____ organizing, comparing, or storing data

3. _____ results printed on paper

4. _____ set of instructions for a computer

5. _____ computer machinery

6. _____ entering data

7. _____ computer programs

8. _____ used for typing in data

Name _____

Sensory words describe something you **see, hear, smell, touch,** or **taste.** Choose a word from the word box that describes each phrase.

steamy	bitter
murmur	deafening
coarse	smooth
dim	fragrant
rustling	screeching

1. grasping steel wool _____

2. a crowd of people yelling _____

3. marble surface _____

4. blooming roses _____

5. unsweetened chocolate _____

6. leaves in the wind _____

7. sitting in a sauna _____

8. an owl in the night _____

Name _____

Match the sense with the sensory word.

see	murmur
touch	dim
hear	bitter
smell	smooth
taste	salty

Write a sentence using each of the sensory words above.

1. _____

2. _____

3. _____

4. _____

5. _____

Name _____

Rewrite each sentence with at least two sensory words.

1. This is my sister.

   _____

2. Have you seen my fish?

   _____

3. I am sad today.

   _____

4. That movie is good.

   _____

5. I saw an animal.

   _____

Name _____

Onomatopoeia is a word that **sounds like the sound** it describes, such as **snap, pop,** and **swish.** Write a poem describing a thunderstorm, the ocean, or an April rain shower using onomatopoeia words.

_____

_____

_____

_____

_____

_____

_____

_____

_____

Name _____

Read the onomatopoeia words. Write a sentence using each word.

1. crunch _____

_____

2. hum _____

_____

3. zonk _____

_____

4. sigh _____

_____

5. snap _____

_____

6. clatter _____

_____

Name _____

A **plural** word is **more than one** of a person, place, or thing. Remember to add **es** to words that end in **x, sh,** and **ch,** to change **y** to **i** and add **es,** and to change **f** to **v** and add **es.** Change each word to the plural form. Write it on the line.

1. The _____ are hiding in the _____.
   squirrel   ditch

2. You will see _____ at many _____.
   seal   beach

3. Put the _____ in the _____.
   firefly   jar

4. How many _____ did you pick from the _____?
   berry   bush

5. Put the _____ in the _____.
   letter   mailbox

6. Put the _____ on the _____.
   brush   shelf

7. I bought two _____ for my _____.
   watch   friend

8. We saw ten _____ on three _____.
   bird   branch

9. I want two _____ for my _____.
   lollipop   sister

10. The _____ are taking their _____.
    baby   nap

Name _____

Make each word plural and write it in the correct column.

Hint: If there's a vowel before the **y**, add **s**.
　　　If there's a consonant, change the **y** to **i** and add **es**.

Add **s**

_____

_____

_____

Change the
y to **i** and add **es**

_____　　　_____

_____　　　_____

_____　　　_____

_____　　　_____

_____

Name _____

Make the following words plural.

1. cranberry   _____

2. bunny   _____

3. calf   _____

4. church   _____

5. rainbow   _____

6. watch   _____

7. life   _____

8. hobby   _____

9. notch   _____

10. vicinity   _____

11. psalm   _____

12. index   _____

13. half   _____

14. suffix   _____

15. symphony   _____

Write the plural of each word in the line. Then write the plural in the correct box puzzle.

1. match _____
2. city _____
3. school _____
4. foot _____
5. body _____
6. church _____
7. man _____
8. radio _____

9. calf _____
10. penny _____
11. child _____
12. piano _____
13. woman _____
14. story _____
15. sandwich _____
16. mouse _____

Name _____

A **suffix** is a word part added to the **end of a word** that changes its meaning.
Use the suffix definitions in the box to write a definition of each word below.

> **ist** means "one who practices"
> **ous** means "full of"
> **ance** means "the state of"

1. artist _____

2. courageous _____

3. admittance _____

4. appearance _____

5. guitarist _____

6. humorous _____

7. inheritance _____

8. mountainous _____

9. poisonous _____

10. violinist _____

Name _____

Add the suffix **ful** or **ly** to the word from the box that makes sense in the sentence.

harm	easy
care	glad
use	brave
rest	sudden
hope	clear

1. Please be _____ when you use the iron.

2. _____ a flock of geese swept across the sky.

3. Our vacation at the beach was so _____.

4. Sandy got an A on her speech because she spoke so _____.

5. Our team is _____ that we will make the playoffs.

6. Some activities are _____ to your health.

7. Manuel _____ climbed the tree to get his sister's escaped parakeet.

8. I will _____ deliver your papers for you while you are gone.

9. Your notes will be _____ as you prepare for the test.

10. The class aced the test _____.

Name _____

Add the suffix **less** or **ness** to complete each sentence.

1. We adopted a home _____ dog from the pound.

2. My favorite thing about the dog is the soft _____ of its fur.

3. The thick _____ of its fur keeps the dog warm.

4. Dark _____ scared our dog at first, so it slept in my brother's room.

5. It was use _____ to try to break the dog of that habit!

6. Our house was never spot _____ before the dog arrived, but it is definitely messy now.

7. Feeling at home with our new pet was pain _____.

8. We were not care _____ when we named our dog.

Name _____

Write the word with a suffix from the word box that fits the definition.

```
        supportive        patience
        absence           intelligence
        truthful          forgetful
        thoughtful        doubtful
        cheerful          active
```

1. thinking carefully _____

2. has trouble remembering _____

3. having a sunny attitude _____

4. keeping busy _____

5. disbelieving or questioning _____

6. always telling the truth _____

7. the state of not being present _____

8. smartness _____

9. showing great care or concern _____

10. ability to wait calmly _____

Name _____

Write the definition of each word using the suffix definitions in the word box.

ness   quality of being
ble   capable of being

1. bleak<u>ness</u> _____

2. permiss<u>ible</u> _____

3. break<u>able</u> _____

4. blind<u>ness</u> _____

5. steadi<u>ness</u> _____

6. admiss<u>ible</u> _____

7. furri<u>ness</u> _____

8. believ<u>able</u> _____

Name _____

Complete each sentence using a word with a suffix from the word box.

collection	invitation
capable	improvements
peaceful	addition
wonderful	marvelous

1. My birthday was_____.

2. This is my _____ of stamps.

3. It is so _____ up in the mountains.

4. In _____ to dance lessons, I take piano and clarinet.

5. The _____ for the wedding came yesterday.

6. The movie was _____!

7. Dad is working on a few home _____.

8. He is not _____ of lifting all those heavy boxes himself.

Name _____

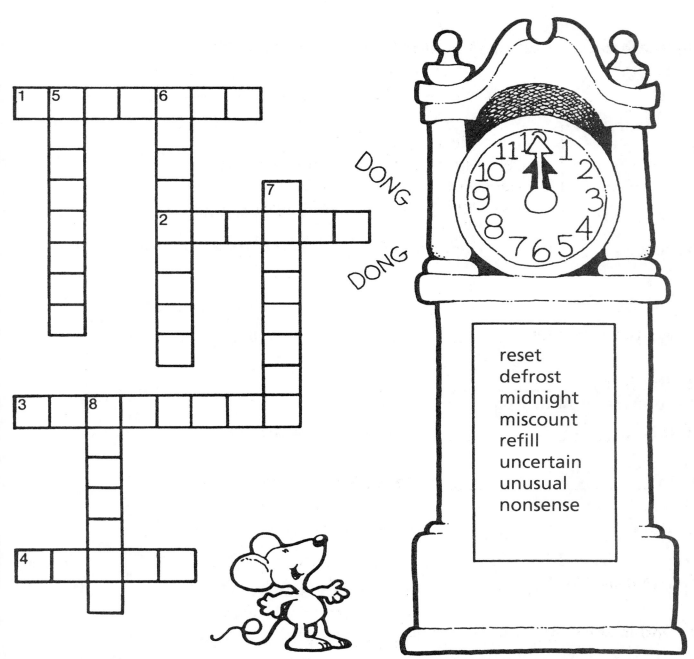

reset
defrost
midnight
miscount
refill
uncertain
unusual
nonsense

A **prefix** is a word part added to the **beginning of a word** that changes its meaning. Match the words in the word box with their definitions below. Write them in the correct places in the puzzle.

Across
1. not usual
2. fill again
3. middle of the night
4. set again

Down
5. not making sense
6. not certain
7. count wrongly
8. take away frost

Name _____

Match each word with its meaning. Write the number of the word by its meaning.

1. exhale   _____ breathe in

2. inhale   _____ breathe out

3. misread   _____ read wrongly

4. reread   _____ read again

5. bicycle   _____ three-wheeled cycle

6. tricycle   _____ two-wheeled cycle

Use the words above to complete the sentences.

1. Allen likes to _____ the fresh mountain air.

2. Carmen is in a _____ race today.

3. The model airplane you put together may not work if you _____ the directions.

4. The baby's _____ is in the garage.

5. Matt wants to _____ this book.

6. Take in a deep breath, then _____.

Name _____

incorrect
ashore
unclear
renew
prepay
imperfect
dislike
mistreat

Match the words in the word box with their definitions below. Write them in the correct places in the puzzle.

Across

1. pay before
2. treat wrongly
3. not correct
4. not clear

Down

5. not like
6. not perfect
7. make new again
8. on shore

Name _____

Match each word with its meaning. Write the number of the word by its meaning.

1. increase   _____ become larger

2. decrease   _____ become smaller

_____

3. indirect   _____ direct again

4. redirect   _____ not direct

_____

5. inflate   _____ to let out air

6. deflate   _____ to blow air into

Use the words above to complete the sentences.

1. When I _____ the tire, it will be flat.

2. To make more soup, _____ the amount of water.

3. Nick took an _____ route to school.

4. If you are lost, a police officer can _____ you.

5. Here are twenty balloons to _____ for the party.

6. The price of shirts will _____ during the big sale.

Name _____

Complete each sentence with a **con** word from the word box.

converged	controversy	contorted	conclude	consult
convince	conduct	conscious	congested	confetti
contrition	contestant	conservation	conjured	

1. The mall was _____ with swarms of sale-crazed customers.

2. Did you _____ your teacher that they are a good group?

3. Please _____ your doctor if your fever continues.

4. Peter's face _____ in pain as his horse stomped on his foot.

5. The two highways _____ before we reached Toronto.

6. Our _____ group hopes to plant 50 trees this Saturday.

7. The tearful toddler, filled with _____, told her dead goldfish that she only meant to take it for a walk.

8. Are you _____, Henry? Speak to me if you can hear me!

9. The brawny guide will _____ us to the bottom of the gorge.

10. Our meeting will _____ in twenty minutes.

11. There was a horrid _____ about the music selection chosen for the skating party.

12. What evil the wicked warlock _____ against his unsuspecting apprentice!

13. When the first _____ could not answer the riddle, he was sentenced to nine years hard dishwashing.

14. After our team won, we tossed _____ high into the air to celebrate.

Name _____

Read the story. Use the prefixes in the word box to write in the missing prefixes.

un	tele	dis	re	mis

Star Trip

As usual, the Little Prince of Mars sat in front of his big-screen

_____(1) vision. "This life is very _____(2) interesting," he thought.

Just then, he heard a knock at the door. When he opened the door, a

messenger handed him a _____(3) gram. "There must be some

_____(4) take," said the Little Prince. But when he opened the envelope,

he was surprised. The _____(5) happy frown on his face _____(6) appeared.

He was going on a trip to the stars! The Little Prince

was _____(7) certain what to pack. He dashed for his _____(8) scope and

magic crystal kit. He packed and _____(9) packed his star travel

bag until everything fit. Someday he would _____(10) turn to his own planet,

but until then, he was ready for an adventure in the stars!

Spectrum Vocabulary Grade 6

Name _____

Many words consist of one or more **Greek** or **Latin root**. For example, the Greek root **tele** means **far**. When it is combined with **vis**, the Latin root for **see**, we get **television**. Fill in the blanks below to learn the meaning of more roots.

1. Telephones allow us to hear sounds from far away. **Tele** means _____, and **phone** comes from the Greek word meaning _____.

2. **Ped** is a root word meaning foot. Therefore, a **pedestrian** is a person who travels by _____.

3. **Graph** comes from the Greek word meaning to write, and **auto** is the root word for self. Thus, an **autograph** is _____ .

4. **Geo** is the Greek root for Earth. **Geography**, then, is writing or drawing about the _____.

5. **Bio** is the root word meaning life. When someone writes an **autobiography**, he or she writes about _____.

6. A **biographer** writes about _____.

7. The word **pedometer** combines the root **ped** with **meter**, a root meaning measurement. A **pedometer** is an instrument for _____ the distance someone travels by _____.

8. **Logy** is a Greek root for study. When combined with the root **graph**, we get **graphology** or the study of _____.

9. **Biology** is the study of _____.

10. **Geology** is the study of _____.

11. Writing that comes from far away is called a _____.

12. Combine the root word for sound and the root for write. The machine we use to play records is a _____.

Name _____

Add new words to your vocabulary by understanding these Greek or Latin roots.

1. **Magna** or **magni** is the Latin root for great. **Magnificent** is an adjective that means excellent or great.

2. **Aqua** is the Latin word meaning water. An **aquarium** is a place for keeping water plants and **aquatic** animals.

3. **Flor** is the Latin root for flower. A **florist** sells or grows flowers for a living.

4. **Dict** is the Latin root meaning to speak. **Diction** means the manner in which words are spoken.

5. **Micro** comes from the Greek word *mikros*, meaning tiny or small. A **microscope** is an instrument that allows us to see very small things.

Use a dictionary to find two words formed from each of the above roots. Write words and their definitions in the blanks below.

root	dictionary word	definition
1. **magna** or **magni**	(a) _____	(a) _____
	(b) _____	(b) _____
2. **aqua**	(a) _____	(a) _____
	(b) _____	(b) _____
3. **flor**	(a) _____	(a) _____
	(b) _____	(b) _____
4. **dict**	(a) _____	(a) _____
	(b) _____	(b) _____
5. **micro**	(a) _____	(a) _____
	(b) _____	(b) _____

Name _____

aqua, aque	water

aqualung	breathing equipment for underwater swimming or diving
aquamarine	a bluish sea-green color
aquaplane	a wide board that is towed by a motorboat, like a single water ski
aquarium	an artificial pond or tank of water where live water animals and water plants are kept; a building where such collections are exhibited
aquatic	growing or living in water
aqueduct	a channel that carries large amounts of water

Divide the following words into parts so that **aqua (or aque)** is separate.

Example: aqua rium

1. aquamarine _____ _____

2. aqualung _____ _____

3. aquaplane _____ _____

4. aqueduct _____ _____

Complete each sentence using a word from the word box.

1. To go scuba diving, you need to wear an _____.

2. The children bought a variety of fish for the _____.

3. Seaweed is an _____ plant.

4. The Romans used an _____ to transport water from one place to another.

5. Susan liked to waterski, but her brother John preferred to use an _____.

Name _____

dict	to say
dictate	to say something aloud that will be written or recorded by another; to command or order
dictator	a ruler with unlimited power
diction	a style of speaking; the degree of preciseness or clarity in speech
predict	to foretell or say ahead of time that something will happen
verdict	a judgment or decision, especially that of a jury in a court case

Circle the root that means **to say** in the following words.

1. diction

2. predict

3. dictator

4. verdict

Complete each sentence using a word from the word box.

1. The foreman of the jury announced the _____: not guilty.

2. The actor was very careful of his _____ during the audition.

3. The manager will _____ the new rules to the employees.

4. I _____ that my little brother will have a dent in his new bike before the end of the week.

Name _____

spec	to see, to look at
aspect	the look or appearance of anything
introspective	examining one's own thoughts and feelings
specimen	a single part or thing used as a sample or example of a whole group
spectacle	anything viewed or seen; a public performance
spectator	a person who watches an event
spectrum	the range of colors visible to the human eye; a continuous range or entire extent

Unscramble these words. Write the correct word next to its meaning.

calcepest   casttrope   pacset   victorinestep   mesnepic

1. the way a person or a thing looks _____

2. a typical part or example _____

3. looking into one's own mind and feelings _____

4. something to look at _____

5. an onlooker _____

Complete each sentence using a word from the word box.

1. The circus advertised itself as the greatest _____ in the world.

2. No one realized he was ever _____, because he always seemed so self-confident.

3. The investigator asked for a _____ of everyone's handwriting.

4. You can find the whole _____ of types in our school—from preppie to punk.

5. In bruising games like football and soccer, I'd rather be a _____ than a participant.

6. Elsie's whole _____ reflected what an absolutely terrible week it had been.

Answer the questions below.

What is a spectator sport? _____

List four spectator sports. _____ _____ _____ _____

Name _____

deca, deci	ten, tenth

decade	a period of ten years
decathlon	an athletic contest in which each contestant participates in ten events
decibel	a unit of sound intensity
decimal	a fraction with an unwritten denominator of ten, indicated by a decimal point before the numerator
decimate	to kill or destroy a large part of (originally, to kill every tenth person)

Fill in each blank with a word from the word box.

1. In the Middle Ages, the Black Plague _____ (ed) the population of Europe.

2. To win a _____, you must excel at ten different sports.

3. The _____ level of the jackhammer hurt my ears.

4. Rhonda can recite the numerical value of pi to the tenth _____.

5. My uncle is 50, so he has lived through five _____ (s).

Answer the questions below.

1. Name five important events in the first decade of your life.

_____

_____

_____

_____

_____

2. Use an encyclopedia or an almanac to compare the decibel levels of a whisper, a jet plane, and rock music. At what level is sound considered painful?

_____

_____

_____

_____

Name _____

circ, circum	around, circle
circa	about or approximately
circuitous	roundabout; indirect; devious
circulation	the act of moving in a circle or circuit or of moving from place to place
circumference	the outer line of a circle; the length of this line
circumnavigate	to sail around something, especially the world
circumscribe	to draw or form a line around, especially a circle; to limit or restrain
circumspect	careful to consider all related circumstances before acting or deciding; cautious
circumvent	to avoid or find a way around

Look up the following words in a dictionary. Briefly define each word in the blank that follows it.

1. circadian   _____

2. circuitry   _____

3. circumflex   _____

4. circumstantial   _____

Fill in each blank with a word from the word box.

1. Johnny came up with some very creative excuses to _____ doing his homework.

2. Ferdinand Magellan's ship was the first to _____ the world.

3. On her first day at the new school, Marie was _____; she wanted to get a sense of the various crowds before she picked new friends.

4. When his parents said he could never stay out past nine o'clock, Arthur felt he was being unreasonably _____(d).

5. The doctor said that my grandmother must find some type of exercise that would help improve the _____ of her blood.

Name _____

ject	to throw
abject	contemptible; humble; wretched
conjecture	a guess or a judgment without sufficient evidence
dejected	sad and depressed
eject	to force out or cause to be removed
interject	to break in with a comment while someone else is speaking
projectile	something thrown or fired through the air
rejection	a refusal to accept or to use
trajectory	the path, especially a curve, traced by a moving object

Fill in each blank with a word from the word box.

1. The tornado turned trees and shingles into dangerous _____ (s).

2. He offered an _____ apology.

3. Just before the plane crashed, the pilot pushed the button that would _____ him.

4. The crowd followed the _____ of the ball as it sailed out of the ballpark.

5. His accusation was based only on _____.

6. "I know the answer," she _____(ed) before the game-show emcee could even finish asking the question.

Circle the root that means **to throw.** Write a sentence using each word.

1. project *(noun)* _____

2. adjective _____

3. injection _____

4. reject *(noun)* _____

5. interjection _____

6. object *(noun)* _____

7. subject *(noun)* _____

Name _____

An **imported word** is an English word that **comes from another language.**

PARLEZ VOUZ FRANÇAIS?

catalogue	carrousel	boulevard	question
bouquet	budget	crayon	menu
lieu	bandage	rare	cinema

Complete each sentence with a French word from the word box.

1. Let's use the skateboard in _____ of the skates.

2. Do you want to ask me a _____ ?

3. I think I need a _____ for this cut.

4. Let's ride our bikes down the _____.

5. Riding the horses on the _____ was great!

6. That is a beautiful _____ of flowers!

7. What movies are playing at the _____ today?

8. Do you have a magenta _____ I can use?

9. Before we decide what to order, let's study the _____.

10. I want to look at the _____ before I decide what clothes to buy.

11. Sticking to a _____ keeps you from spending too much.

12. That albino snake is very _____.

Name _____

Throughout history, English-speaking people have borrowed words from other languages. Many dictionaries give an **etymology** or short word history to tell the origin of a word.

Look up the following list of words in a dictionary. Write the definition beside the word.

1. **comrade** (from Spanish) _____

2. **caravan** (from Persian) _____

3. **bungalow** (from Hindi) _____

4. **scant** (from Danish) _____

5. **solo** (from Italian) _____

6. **clan** (from Gaelic) _____

Use the words from above to complete the following sentences.

7. My grandparents live in a new _____ near the mountains.

8. The _____ rations were not enough to feed the campers.

9. The girl will sing a _____ at the talent show.

10. The hiker helped his _____ climb up the steep slope.

11. The four families are all members of the same _____ in Scotland.

12. The truck drivers formed a _____ for the long drive through the desert.

Name _____

Native Americans introduced European explorers and settlers to many new and wonderful things. For example, Europeans had never seen a moose or a skunk before. They had never tasted foods such as squash nor had they ridden in sturdy, lightweight boats called *canoes*. The Native American words for all these new sights eventually became part of the English language, along with the Native names of many places.

tepee	toboggan	pecan	Alaska
opossum	Texas	Alabama	raccoon
Canada	Michigan	hickory	moccasin

Below is a list of Native American words and their meanings. Write the English words from the word box beside the corresponding Native American term.

Native American Word	Meaning	English Word
1. tejas	friends, allies	_____
2. kanata	village	_____
3. aposoum	white animal	_____
4. alayeska	great land	_____
5. pacane	hard-shelled nut	_____
6. michigama	great lake	_____
7. topagan	drag made of skin	_____
8. aroughcun	scratcher	_____
9. pocahiquara	food made from pounded nuts	_____
10. mokkussin	shoe	_____
11. alibamu	I clear the thicket	_____
12. tipi	ti — to dwell pi — to use for	_____

Name _____

January was named for Janus, the Roman god of doors, who had a face that looked to the past and one that looked to the future.

February came from the Latin word *februare*, which means *to purify*. During this month, the Romans purified themselves for festivals.

March was named for Mars, the Roman god of war.

April may have gotten its name from the Latin word *aperire*, which means *to open*, or from Aphrodite, the Greek goddess of love.

May was named for Maia, the Roman goddess of spring.

June is thought to have been named for Juno, the Roman goddess of marriage.

July was named in honor of Julius Caesar, a Roman statesman born in this month.

August was named in honor of the Roman emperor Augustus.

September came from the Latin word *septem*, which means *seven*. In the old Roman calendar, September was the seventh month.

October came from the Latin word *octo* for *eight*. October was once the eighth month.

November came from the Latin word *novem*, which means *nine*. In the old Roman calendar, November was the ninth month.

December was named after the Latin word *decem*, which means *ten*. In the old Roman calendar, December was the tenth month.

Complete the puzzle using the words and their definitions in the word box.

Across

2. Named for Juno
5. Goddess of Spring
7. Comes from a Latin word meaning *nine*
9. Latin word for *seven*
11. Caesar, a Roman statesman

Down

1. Meaning of decem
2. God of doors
3. A month for purifying
4. Named for goddess of love
6. Named for a Roman emperor
8. Latin word for *eight*
10. God of war

Name _____

Read the chart to find out where the names for the days of the week came from.

Modern English	Old English	Meaning	
Sunday	Sunnandaeg	*day of the sun*	Named in honor of the sun
Monday	Monandaeg	*day of the moon*	Named in honor of the moon
Tuesday	Tiwesdaeg	*Tyr's day*	Named after Tyr, the norse god of war
Wednesday	Wodnesdaeg	*Woden's day*	Named after Woden, the chief god in Norse mythology
Thursday	Thuresdaeg	*Thor's day*	Named after Thor, the Norse god of thunder
Friday	Frigedaeg	*Frigg's day*	Named after Frigg, the Norse goddess of love and Woden's wife
Saturday	Saeter-daeg	*Saturn's day*	Named after Saturn, the Roman god of agriculture

Write the days of the week in Modern English.

1. Thuresdaeg _____

2. Wodnesdaeg _____

3. Sunnandaeg _____

4. Saeter-daeg _____

5. Monandaeg _____

6. Frigedaeg _____

7. Tiwesdaeg _____

Answer the questions. Use the Old English term for the days of the week.

8. What day is today? _____

9. What day is tomorrow? _____

10. What day is the last day of this month? _____

11. On what day does your birthday fall this year? _____

12. On what day do you stay up the latest? _____

Name _____

The myths of the ancient Greeks and Romans were filled with powerful gods and goddesses. The names of these supernatural beings became the sources of many English words.

Write the name of the Greek god or goddess who inspired each of the words below.

1. **cereal**—different types of grain

   _____

2. **geology**—the study of the history of the earth

   _____

3. **museum**—a place where works of art are displayed

   _____

4. **hypnosis**—a method of putting people in a state that resembles sleep

   _____

Ceres —	Roman goddess of the harvest
Gaea —	Greek goddess of the earth
Hypnos —	Greek god of sleep
Jove —	another name for Jupiter, king of the gods in Roman mythology
Muses —	Greek goddesses of art and science
Pan —	Greek god of the woods who was able to fill people with sudden terror
Titans —	a family of giants in Greek mythology

5. **panic**—a feeling of strong, uncontrollable fear _____

6. **jovial**—jolly, happy _____

7. **titanic**—huge, powerful _____

Fill in the blanks with the **boldfaced** words above.

8. We saw a colorful painting at the _____.

9. Our class studied _____ and learned about how different types of rocks formed.

10. A person under _____ sometimes looks asleep.

11. What kind of _____ do you enjoy for breakfast?

12. My Aunt Julie is so _____ that we call her Aunt Jolly.

13. The wave that swept the shore during last year's storm was _____!

14. It is important not to _____ when you are in danger.

Abbreviations are **the shortened version** of a word.

Rewrite Yuki's birthday invitation using abbreviations.

What: Yuki's Eleventh Birthday Party

_____

When: Saturday, January Tenth

_____

Where: Seven Hundred Eighty Six Maple Boulevard

_____

Rewrite the directions to Yuki's house without the abbreviations.

1. Take MLK Jr. Hwy to Rt. 7. Turn rt.

_____

2. Go 4 mi. to 1st light. Turn rt.

_____

3. Maple Blvd. is the 2nd St. on the lt.

_____

4. 786 is the 3rd house on the rt.

_____

Name _____

Rewrite Isabel's planner entries without **abbreviations**. Check the word box for help with abbreviations you don't know.

cash on	building
delivery	meeting
appointment	dozen

1. Dentist appt. Sat. Feb. 2

_____

2. soccer booster mtg. Mon. after school

_____

3. Fri. May 6 camping trip—meet at Bldg.2

_____

4. 1st soccer game Tues. Apr 11

_____

5. pick up doz. roses for Mother's Day May 13.

_____

6. deliver fund raiser candy, c.o.d.

_____

Name _____

Rewrite each statement without abbreviations.

Celsius	millimeter
inch	pound
yard	centimeter
ounces	mile
foot	dozen
Fahrenheit	

1. 3 ft. make 1 yd.

_____

2. 12 in. make 1 ft.

_____

3. there are 16 oz. in 1 lb.

_____

4. 1 doz. is made of 12 objects

_____

5. there are 5280 ft. in 1 mi.

_____

6. there are 1760 yd. in 1 mi.

_____

7. there are 100 mm in 1 cm

_____

8. 32 degrees F is equal to 0 degrees C

_____

Name _____

Match each abbreviation to its meaning.

1. Rd. _____   A.   ante meridiem (before noon)

2. B.C. _____   B.   parkway

3. A.D. _____   C.   post office

4. A.M. _____   D.   rural route or railroad

5. P.M. _____   E.   road

6. St. _____   F.   avenue

7. Pkwy. _____   G.   drive or doctor

8. S.E. _____   H.   post meridiem (after noon)

9. Ln. _____   I.   mount or mountain

10. R.R. _____   J.   before Christ

11. Mt. _____   K.   lane

12. P.O. _____   L.   street

13. Ave. _____   M.   anno Domini (in the year of the Lord)

14. Blvd. _____   N.   miles per hour

15. m.p.h. _____   O.   northeast

16. N.W. _____   P.   southwest

17. S.W. _____   Q.   miles per gallon

18. N.E. _____   R.   northwest

19. Dr. _____   S.   southeast

20. m.p.g. _____   T.   boulevard

Name _____

A **compound word** combines **two words to make a new word.**

Write a word from the bubbles on each line to form a compound word.

1. _____ fire

2. _____ stick

3. _____ comb

4. _____ land

5. _____ sack

6. _____ wood

7. _____ giving

8. _____ top

9. _____ corn

10. _____ melon

11. _____ storm

12. _____ blazer

13. _____ suds

14. _____ blower

15. _____ hook

16. _____ paste

Name _____

Write a sentence for each compound word you formed on page 77.

1. _____

2. _____

3. _____

4. _____

5. _____

6. _____

7. _____

8. _____

9. _____

10. _____

11. _____

12. _____

13. _____

14. _____

15. _____

16. _____

Name _____

Look at each picture clue below. Write the compound word it represents.

1.

_____

2.

_____

3.

_____

4.

_____

5.

_____

6.

_____

7.

_____

8.

_____

Name _____

Combine the first number from Set A with the second number from Set B to make a compound word.

 Set A

 Set B

Set A		Set B	
1. after	7. grape	1. work	7. writer
2. black	8. cheese	2. out	8. case
3. bare	9. skate	3. burger	9. noon
4. ginger	10. type	4. light	10. fruit
5. flash	11. pillow	5. basket	11. board
6. home	12. waste	6. foot	12. bread

Example:

1 + 9 = afternoon

8 + 3 =

5 + 4 =

7 + 10 =

2 + 2 =

12 + 5 =

11 + 8 =

6 + 1 =

10 + 7 =

4 + 12 =

9 + 11 =

3 + 6 =

Name _____

Choose a word from the list on the right to combine with a word on the left to form a compound word.

Example:

<u>M</u>   1. chalk   <u>chalkboard</u>   a. piece

_____ 2. over   _____   b. foot

_____ 3. tooth   _____   c. cycle

_____ 4. apple   _____   d. mint

_____ 5. post   _____   e. due

_____ 6. bare   _____   f. down

_____ 7. ear   _____   g. spoon

_____ 8. mouth   _____   h. work

_____ 9. water   _____   i. sauce

_____ 10. table   _____   j. melon

_____ 11. motor   _____   k. right

_____ 12. wall   _____   l. house

_____ 13. count   _____   m. board

_____ 14. light   _____   n. bread

_____ 15. pepper   _____   o. tub

_____ 16. basket   _____   p. mark

_____ 17. ginger   _____   q. ball

_____ 18. copy   _____   r. ache

_____ 19. bath   _____   s. paper

_____ 20. home   _____   t. pick

Name _____

Use a word from word box 1 and a word from word box 2 to make a compound word for each meaning. Write the compound word.

1. something to drink _____

2. an animal _____

3. an insect _____

4. a direction _____

5. place for dishes _____

6. a meal _____

7. behind house _____

8. for letters _____

9. for plants _____

10. where you sleep _____

Word Box 1		Word Box 2	
cup	flower	shake	room
milk	back	cat	board
bed	butter	fly	fast
north	mail	east	yard
wild	break	pot	box

PAGE 4

Classification means to put words together in **groups**. A word **analogy** expresses the **relationship between words**. Complete each analogy with an appropriate word.

1. Cup is to adult as bottle is to __baby__
2. Four is to dog as two is to __human (answers may vary)__
3. Skin is to human as feathers are to __birds__
4. Paw is to dog as hoof is to __horse__
5. Hot is to oven as cold is to __freezer__
6. Watch is to wrist as ring is to __finger__
7. Round is to ball as square is to __block__
8. Calf is to cow as foal is to __horse__
9. Antlers are to deer as horns are to __bull__
10. Ink is to pen as paint is to __brush__
11. Rain is to spring as snow is to __winter__
12. Tadpole is to frog as caterpillar is to __butterfly__

PAGE 5

Two of the most common analogies involve synonyms and antonyms.

Model 1: *Word* is to *word* as *word* is to _____.
        (synonym)   (synonym)
Example: *Small* is to *little* as *big* is to *large*.

Model 2: *Word* is to *word* as *word* is to _____.
        (antonym)   (antonym)
Example: *Beautiful* is to *ugly* as *happy* is to *sad*.

Read the definitions of the words in the word box. Complete the analogies below using words from the word box.

timid—*adj.* without courage   **jovial**—*adj.* full of laughter, jolly
sullen—*adj.* gloomy, bad humored   **climate**—*n.* weather conditions
foe—*n.* enemy   **loathe**—*v.* to dislike, to detest
bold—*adj.* showing great courage   **comprehend**—*v.* to understand

1. *Bad* is to *terrible* as *shy* is to __timid__
2. *Bad* is to *good* as __foe__ is to *friend*.
3. *Car* is to *automobile* as *weather* is to __climate__
4. *Teach* is to *instruct* as *understand* is to __comprehend__
5. *Shout* is to *whisper* as *love* is to __loathe__
6. *Mean* is to *kind* as *shy* is to __bold__
7. *Gentle* is to *rough* as *happy* is to __sullen__
8. *Pretty* is to *cute* as __jovial__ is to *jolly*.
9. *Love* is to *like* as __loathe__ is to *detest*.
10. *Bush* is to *shrub* as *enemy* is to __foe__

PAGE 6

Read the analogy models, then circle the correct word to complete each analogy below. Use a dictionary if you need help.

Model 1: *Tool* is to its *function* as *tool* is to its _____.
        (function)
Example: *Pen* is to *writing* as *shovel* is to *digging*.

Model 2: *Title* is to *specialty* as *title* is to _____.
        (specialty)
Example: *Dentist* is to *teeth* as *veterinarian* is to *animals*.

Model 3: *Cause* is to *effect* as *cause* is to _____.
        (effect)
Example: *Sadness* is to *tears* as *joy* is to *laughter*.

Model 4: *Worker* is to *product* as *worker* is to _____.
        (product)
Example: *Author* is to *book* as *artist* is to *painting*.

1. *Policeman* is to *crime* as *doctor* is to _____.
   a. illness b. nurse c. stethoscope d. patient
2. *Carpenter* is to *hammer* as *doctor* is to _____.
   a. illness b. nurse c. stethoscope d. patient
3. *Druggist* is to *pharmacy* as *teacher* is to _____.
   a. student b. school c. books d. teach
4. *Baker* is to *bread* as *seamstress* is to _____.
   a. thread b. needle c. dress d. sewing
5. *Scissors* are to *cut* as *ax* is to _____.
   a. chop b. burn c. tree d. sharpen
6. *Sun* is to *sunburn* as *snow* is to _____.
   a. overcast b. frostbite c. umbrella d. climate
7. *Fire* is to *burn* as *cold* is to _____.
   a. ice b. freeze c. snow d. wind
8. *Hunger* is to *eat* as *thirst* is to _____.
   a. food b. cup c. milk d. drink

PAGE 7

Look up each of the following words in a dictionary and write the definitions on the line. Then, use these words to complete each analogy below.

1. **punctual** __on time, prompt__
2. **fragile** __easily broken, delicate__
3. **discard** __to throw out or sway, cast off__
4. **fraudulent** __cheating, dishonest__
5. **peril** __the condition of being in danger__
6. **prohibit** __to not allow by law__
7. **monotonous** __not interesting because of repetition__
8. **decade** __a unit o time equaling 10 years__
9. **augment** __to make greater in size or amount__
10. **soothe** __to make less angry__
11. *Food* is to *eat* as *trash* is to __discard__
12. *Late* is to *early* as *tardy* is to __punctual__
13. *Metal* is to *sturdy* as *glass* is to __fragile__
14. *Accept* is to *reject* as *allow* is to __prohibit__
15. *Loud* is to *quiet* as *varied* is to __monotonous__
16. *Real* is to *genuine* as *fake* is to __fraudulent__
17. *One hundred* is to *century* as *ten* is to __decade__
18. *Hard* is to *soft* as *disturb* is to __soothe__
19. *Take* is to *give* as *subtract* is to __augment__
20. *Walk* is to *stroll* as *danger* is to __peril__

PAGE 8

Classify each animal from the word box. Write it in the correct column.

Vertebrates (backbones)	Invertebrates (no backbones)
1. ostrich	1. starfish
2. moose	2. octopus
3. Great Dane	3. sand dollar
4. woodpecker	4. jellyfish
5. blue whale	5. sponge
6. aardvark	6. glowworm
7. gerbil	7. butterfly
8. sailfish	8. praying mantis
9. warthog	9. mosquito
10. horned toad	10. earthworm
11. sting ray	11. cicada
12. king snake	12. snail

starfish	horned toad	mosquito	gerbil
ostrich	praying mantis	blue whale	sponge
octopus	sting ray	aardvark	jellyfish
cicada	Great Dane	king snake	sailfish
moose	woodpecker	butterfly	warthog
snail	earthworm	glowworm	sand dollar

PAGE 9

Each word in Bank A shares a feature with a word in Bank B. Place each word with its appropriate feature. Then write another word which shares this feature.

Feature	Bank A word	Bank B word	Your Word
1. sense organ	ear	nose	eye
2. inventor	Edison	Carver	
3. fabric	cotton	polyester	
4. to be read	newspaper	magazine	
5. city	Denver	Santa Fe	
6. direction	north	south	
7. musical genre	rock	jazz	
8. disease	chicken pox	strep throat	
9. color	fuchsia	turquoise	
10. in Washington, D.C.	Smithsonian	Lincoln Memorial	
11. school subject	history	English	
12. body of water	Nile River	Chesapeake Bay	
13. Shakespearean character	Romeo	Hamlet	
14. communication tool	telephone	telegraph	
15. South American country	Bolivia	Paraguay	

Answers may vary.

Bank A: Bolivia, chicken pox, cotton, Denver, Edison, fuchsia, newspaper, Nile River, north, rock, Romeo, Smithsonian, history, telephone

Bank B: Carver, Chesapeake Bay, Hamlet, jazz, Lincoln Memorial, magazine, Paraguay, polyester, English, Santa Fe, south, strep throat, telegraph, turquoise

PAGE 10

Write a word from the word box next to its synonym.

refuse	occur	shake	choose
purchase	fright	rough	reply
copy	vacant	worth	pledge
genuine	depart	simple	tardy

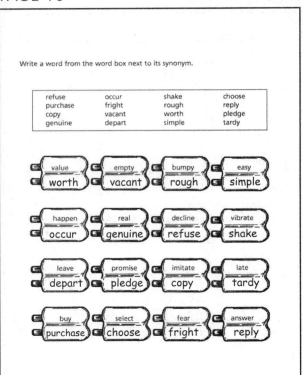

value → worth	empty → vacant	bumpy → rough	easy → simple
happen → occur	real → genuine	decline → refuse	vibrate → shake
leave → depart	promise → pledge	imitate → copy	late → tardy
buy → purchase	select → choose	fear → fright	answer → reply

PAGE 11

Read each sentence carefully. Write the word that best completes each sentence on the line.

1. When my friends gave me a surprise birthday party, I was so surprised that I was **speechless** (synonym for quiet).
   shy · speechless · peaceful

2. She was so **shy** (synonym for quiet) that she couldn't speak in front of the class.
   shy · speechless · peaceful

3. We love going to the mountain cabin because it is so **peaceful** (synonym for quiet) there.
   shy · speechless · peaceful

4. The meat was so **tough** (synonym for hard) that I could barely chew it.
   tough · difficult · firm

5. The test was so **difficult** (synonym for hard) that everyone failed.
   tough · difficult · firm

6. I didn't sleep well because the mattress was too **firm** (synonym for hard).
   tough · difficult · firm

7. He is sure to get a good grade on that **easy** (synonym for simple) test.
   plain · humble · easy

8. The girl was wearing a very **plain** (synonym for simple) blue dress.
   plain · humble · easy

9. The home of the poor farmer was quite **humble** (synonym for simple).
   plain · humble · easy

PAGE 12

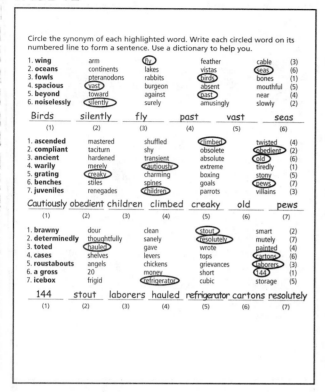

Circle the synonym of each highlighted word. Write each circled word on its numbered line to form a sentence. Use a dictionary to help you.

1. **wing**	arm	(fly)	feather	cable	(3)
2. **oceans**	continents	lakes	vistas	(seas)	(6)
3. **fowls**	pteranodons	rabbits	(birds)	bones	(1)
4. **spacious**	(vast)	burgeon	absent	mouthful	(5)
5. **beyond**	toward	against	(past)	near	(4)
6. **noiselessly**	(silently)	surely	amusingly	slowly	(2)

Birds (1) silently (2) fly (3) past (4) vast (5) seas (6)

1. **ascended**	mastered	shuffled	(climbed)	twisted	(4)
2. **compliant**	taciturn	shy	obsolete	(obedient)	(2)
3. **ancient**	hardened	transient	absolute	(old)	(6)
4. **warily**	merely	(cautiously)	extreme	tiredly	(1)
5. **grating**	(creaky)	charming	boxing	stony	(5)
6. **benches**	stiles	spines	goals	(pews)	(7)
7. **juveniles**	renegades	(children)	parrots	villains	(3)

Cautiously (1) obedient (2) children (3) climbed (4) creaky (5) old (6) pews (7)

1. **brawny**	dour	clean	(stout)	smart	(2)
2. **determinedly**	thoughtfully	sanely	(resolutely)	mutely	(7)
3. **toted**	(hauled)	gave	wrote	painted	(4)
4. **cases**	shelves	levers	tops	(cartons)	(6)
5. **roustabouts**	angels	chickens	grievances	(laborers)	(3)
6. **a gross**	20	(money)	short	(144)	(1)
7. **icebox**	frigid	(refrigerator)	cubic	storage	(5)

144 (1) stout (2) laborers (3) hauled (4) refrigerator (5) cartons (6) resolutely (7)

PAGE 13

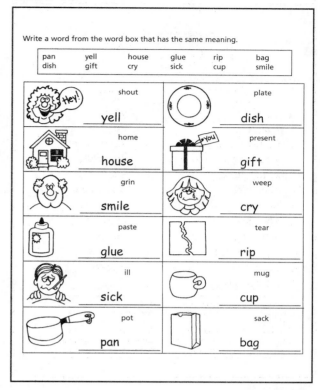

Write a word from the word box that has the same meaning.

pan	yell	house	glue	rip	bag
dish	gift	cry	sick	cup	smile

shout — **yell**		plate — **dish**
home — **house**		present — **gift**
grin — **smile**		weep — **cry**
paste — **glue**		tear — **rip**
ill — **sick**		mug — **cup**
pot — **pan**		sack — **bag**

PAGE 14

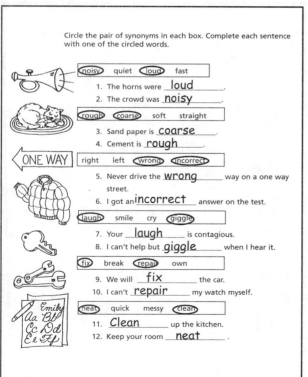

Circle the pair of synonyms in each box. Complete each sentence with one of the circled words.

(noisy) quiet (loud) fast
1. The horns were **loud**.
2. The crowd was **noisy**.

(rough) (coarse) soft straight
3. Sand paper is **coarse**.
4. Cement is **rough**.

right left (wrong) (incorrect)
5. Never drive the **wrong** way on a one way street.
6. I got an **incorrect** answer on the test.

(laugh) smile cry (giggle)
7. Your **laugh** is contagious.
8. I can't help but **giggle** when I hear it.

(fix) break (repair) own
9. We will **fix** the car.
10. I can't **repair** my watch myself.

(neat) quick messy (clean)
11. **Clean** up the kitchen.
12. Keep your room **neat**.

PAGE 15

Antonyms are words that mean the **opposite.** Write the antonym for each word below.

1. near — **far**
2. easy — **difficult/hard**
3. first — **last**
4. high — **low**
5. stand — **sit/lay**
6. best — **worst**
7. boy — **girl**
8. left — **right**
9. question — **answer**
10. north — **south**
11. huge — **tiny**
12. organized — **disorganized**

PAGE 16

Write the antonym for the underlined word in each sentence. Use the words from the word box.

tough	easy
peaceful	talkative
outgoing	difficult
flashy	soft
full	

1. I was <u>speechless</u> when I got up to give my speech. — **talkative**

2. I felt <u>shy</u> as the new girl at the party. — **outgoing**

3. Our neighbor's dogs make the neighborhood so <u>noisy</u>. — **peaceful**

4. The over-cooked steak was <u>soft</u>. — **tough**

5. Can you help me with these <u>easy</u> questions? — **difficult**

6. My pillow is extra <u>firm</u>. — **soft**

7. That test was so <u>difficult</u>! — **easy**

8. The theater was <u>empty</u> for Friday's new release. — **full**

9. That striped and polka-dotted shirt you're wearing sure is <u>plain</u>. — **flashy**

PAGE 17

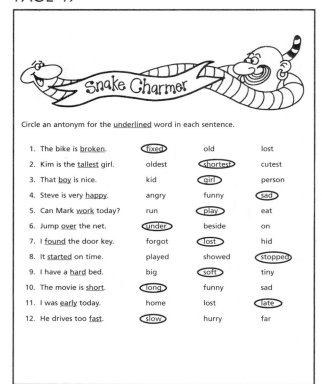

Circle an antonym for the underlined word in each sentence.

1. The bike is <u>broken</u>. — **fixed** · old · lost
2. Kim is the <u>tallest</u> girl. — oldest · **shortest** · cutest
3. That <u>boy</u> is nice. — kid · **girl** · person
4. Steve is very <u>happy</u>. — angry · funny · **sad**
5. Can Mark <u>work</u> today? — run · **play** · eat
6. Jump <u>over</u> the net. — **under** · beside · on
7. I <u>found</u> the door key. — forgot · **lost** · hid
8. It <u>started</u> on time. — played · showed · **stopped**
9. I have a <u>hard</u> bed. — big · **soft** · tiny
10. The movie is <u>short</u>. — **long** · funny · sad
11. I was <u>early</u> today. — home · lost · **late**
12. He drives too <u>fast</u>. — **slow** · hurry · far

PAGE 18

Write the matching antonym for each word.

innocent	present	interior	victory	doubt	rare
defense	increase	shallow	few	wild	plain
departure	minimum	excited	lazy	smooth	rude

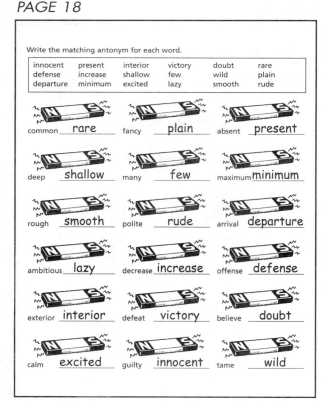

common — **rare**   fancy — **plain**   absent — **present**

deep — **shallow**   many — **few**   maximum — **minimum**

rough — **smooth**   polite — **rude**   arrival — **departure**

ambitious — **lazy**   decrease — **increase**   offense — **defense**

exterior — **interior**   defeat — **victory**   believe — **doubt**

calm — **excited**   guilty — **innocent**   tame — **wild**

PAGE 19

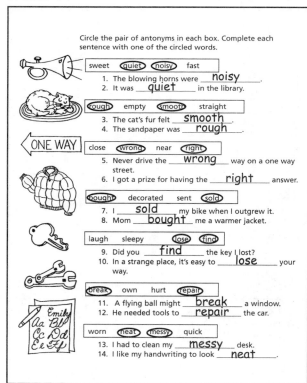

Circle the pair of antonyms in each box. Complete each sentence with one of the circled words.

sweet · **quiet** · **noisy** · fast
1. The blowing horns were **noisy**.
2. It was **quiet** in the library.

rough · empty · **smooth** · straight
3. The cat's fur felt **smooth**.
4. The sandpaper was **rough**.

close · **wrong** · near · **right**
5. Never drive the **wrong** way on a one way street.
6. I got a prize for having the **right** answer.

bought · decorated · sent · **sold**
7. I **sold** my bike when I outgrew it.
8. Mom **bought** me a warmer jacket.

laugh · sleepy · **lose** · **find**
9. Did you **find** the key I lost?
10. In a strange place, it's easy to **lose** your way.

break · own · hurt · **repair**
11. A flying ball might **break** a window.
12. He needed tools to **repair** the car.

worn · **neat** · **messy** · quick
13. I had to clean my **messy** desk.
14. I like my handwriting to look **neat**.

PAGE 20

Read these different meanings for the word **scale** and answer the questions.

1) thin plates on reptiles or fish
2) an object used to measure weight
3) to climb up the side
4) a map marking for distance
5) a group of musical notes

1. Which meaning of scale (1, 2, 3, 4, or 5) does each picture show?

⑤ ② ① ④ ③

2. Choose the correct meaning of **scale** in each sentence. Write the meaning on the line below the sentence.

A. The **scale** shows that the town is 15 miles away.
a map marking for distance

B. Many dinosaurs had **scales**.
thin plates on reptiles or fish

C. I can play **scales** on the piano.
a group of musical notes

D. She put the meat on a **scale**.
an object to measure weight

E. He **scaled** the high mountain.
to climb up the side

PAGE 21

Read the list below.

sign	1) a symbol	2) to write your name
dash	1) a small amount	2) to run quickly
chief	1) leader	2) first or main
trip	1) journey	2) to stumble
quarter	1) one-fourth	2) 25 cent coin
company	1) visitor or guests	2) business

Decide which meaning the **boldfaced** word has in each sentence below. Fill in ① or ②. Then write the meaning on the line.

① ● A. Be careful not to **trip** over the rock!
to stumble

● ② B. We are having **company** tonight.
visitor or guests

① ● C. When it started to rain, we made a **dash** for the house.
to run quickly

● ② D. They turned left at the stop **sign**.
a symbol

① ● E. Mom gave me a **quarter** for my piggy bank.
25 cent coin

● ② F. The **chief** of police spoke to us about safety.
leader

PAGE 22

Write the correct homonym in the matching room of the Homonym Hotel.

HOMONYM HOTEL

8.	1.	7.	13.	14.
12.	3.	11.	6.	5.
4.	2.	9.	10.	

1. The state of Nevada is mostly (desert, dessert).
2. The family went to Virginia (Beech, Beach).
3. The camper's letter began, (Dear, Deer) Mom and Dad.
4. They visited the (Capital, Capitol) building in Washington, D.C.
5. She (road, rode) the roller coaster four times!
6. (There, Their) minivan had a flat tire.
7. (Meet, Meat) me by the diving board at 3:00.
8. The prince sat on his royal (thrown, throne).
9. The elephants at the zoo (paste, paced) back and forth.
10. We (new, knew) our vacation would be in August.
11. Have you ever (bin, been) to New York City?
12. Our dinner was prepared in a Japanese (walk, wok).
13. Our (principle, principal) vacationed in Florida.
14. We toured an old English (manor, manner).

PAGE 23

Circle the homonyms that were misused in the story. Rewrite the story using the correct words.

Four to weaks eye have ben baking cakes with read icing. Ewe can knot waist flower and sugar, sew eye eight every won of the cakes. Of coarse my waste is getting bigger. Eye am getting as big as a hoarse. The plane fact is, I blue my diet.

For two weeks, I have been baking cakes with red icing. I can not waste flour and sugar, so I ate every one of the cakes. Of course, my waist is getting bigger. I am getting as big as a horse. The plain fact is, I blew my diet.

PAGE 24

Circle the homonyms that were misused in the story. Rewrite the story using the correct words.

Land of His Own
The cowboy (rode) his horse into town. He didn't (waist) any time getting there. He went to the bank to get a (lone). He had to (weigh) awhile. But soon he had money to (by) land of his own!

Land of His Own

The cowboy rode his horse into town.
He didn't waste any time getting
there. He went to the bank to get a
loan. He had to wait awhile. But soon
he had money to buy land of his own!

PAGE 25

Circle each misused homonym and write the correct form on the lines below.

One (mourning) while (weighting) (four) the school bus, I felt a (pane) in my (heal). It (seams) I had a (whole) (inn) my shoe and a (peace) of glass was (cot) inside.

1. morning
2. waiting
3. for
4. pain
5. heel
6. seems
7. hole
8. in
9. piece
10. caught

PAGE 26

A **context clue** is a clue or **hint from the sentence** that helps you to figure out words that you don't know. Read each sentence carefully. Guess the definition of each underlined word based on the context clues in the sentence. Then use a dictionary to see how good your guess was.

1. He didn't want to miss that game because the coach had said it was a crucial one in deciding the championship.

    Answers may vary.   very important
    your guess   dictionary definition

2. Although he tried to be punctual, he was always late.

    Answers may vary.   on time
    your guess   dictionary definition

3. The confusing instructions that come with some home computers perplex many people.

    Answers may vary.   puzzle, complicated
    your guess   dictionary definition

4. Light has a velocity of about 186,000 miles per second.

    Answers may vary.   speed
    your guess   dictionary definition

5. Our pet bird warbles happily in his cage all day long.

    Answers may vary.   to sing or whistle
    your guess   dictionary definition

PAGE 27

Read each sentence. Guess the definition of the underlined word. Use a dictionary to check your guesses.

1. I get sunburned easily, so I shun long days at the beach.

    Answers may vary.   to keep away from
    your guess   dictionary definition

2. He skied so well that no one could believe he was a novice.

    Answers may vary.   a person with little experience
    your guess   dictionary definition

3. We grew too many tomatoes, so we gave the surplus to the neighbors.

    Answers may vary.   extra
    your guess   dictionary definition

4. Our teacher berated us for being rude to the guest.

    Answers may vary.   to scold
    your guess   dictionary definition

5. A promise of something for nothing is usually a fraud.

    Answers may vary.   the use of lies to take advantage
    your guess   dictionary definition

6. His anguish over his dog's death did not stop for many weeks.

    Answers may vary.   terrible pain
    your guess   dictionary definition

7. If we want to stay on the team, we must adhere to the rules.

    Answers may vary.   to stick
    your guess   dictionary definition

8. If our best hitter is ill, our chance of winning will diminish.

    Answers may vary.   to make smaller
    Your guess   dictionary definition

PAGE 28

Read each sentence. Guess the definition of the <u>underlined</u> word. Use a dictionary to check your guesses.

1. You will get a ticket from the policeman if you <u>exceed</u> the speed limit.
   <u>Answers may vary.</u>   <u>to go beyond</u>
   your guess   dictionary definition

2. The park ranger asked us to <u>discard</u> our litter in the basket.
   <u>Answers may vary.</u> <u>to throw out or away</u>
   your guess   dictionary definition

3. Although he was in great <u>peril</u>, he risked his life to save the child.
   <u>Answers may vary.</u> <u>the condition of being in danger</u>
   your guess   dictionary definition

4. That is a <u>fragile</u> vase, so please handle it with care.
   <u>Answers may vary.</u> <u>easily broken, delicate</u>
   your guess   dictionary definition

5. He didn't go to the dentist because he feared <u>excruciating</u> pain.
   <u>Answers may vary.</u>   <u>very painful</u>
   your guess   dictionary definition

6. The rain made your note <u>illegible,</u> so we did not know where you had gone.
   <u>Answers may vary.</u> <u>difficult or impossible to read</u>
   your guess   dictionary definition

7. She has purchased many new stamps to <u>augment</u> her collection.
   <u>Answers may vary.</u> <u>make greater in size or amount</u>
   your guess   dictionary definition

8. The <u>obstinate</u> mule refused to budge from the street.
   <u>Answers may vary.</u>   <u>not willing to change</u>
   your guess   dictionary definition

PAGE 29

Read each sentence. Guess the definition of the <u>underlined</u> word. Use a dictionary to check your guesses.

1. His <u>monotonous</u> speech made half the audience fall asleep.
   <u>Answers may vary.</u> <u>not interesting because of repetition</u>
   your guess   dictionary definition

2. The fire department <u>prohibits</u> the use of candles in this theatre because of the fire danger.
   <u>Answers may vary.</u> <u>to not allow by law</u>
   your guess   dictionary definition

3. Her <u>cordial</u> welcome made all her guests feel at home.
   <u>Answers may vary.</u> <u>warm and friendly</u>
   your guess   dictionary definition

4. After the long hike, we all suffered from <u>fatigue</u>.
   <u>Answers may vary.</u> <u>the condition of being tired</u>
   your guess   dictionary definition

5. The elephant looked <u>enormous</u> to the small boy.
   <u>Answers may vary.</u>   <u>huge</u>
   your guess   dictionary definition

6. The snow <u>glistened</u> like jewels in the moonlight.
   <u>Answers may vary.</u> <u>to shine or sparkle</u>
   your guess   dictionary definition

7. Yesterday was a very <u>hectic</u> day because our relatives arrived from Alaska and the dog had puppies on the couch.
   <u>Answers may vary.</u>   <u>marked by hurry</u>
   your guess   dictionary definition

8. When the man lost all his money, he became a <u>pauper</u>.
   <u>Answers may vary.</u> <u>a very poor person</u>
   your guess   dictionary definition

PAGE 30

For each sentence, circle the pair of words that completes the meaning of the sentence.

1. Their profits have been _____, and they wish to _____ their situation.
   a. decreasing—excuse
   b. declining—remedy
   c. comfortable—redress

2. Rats provide a _____ in reducing garbage, but this is outweighed by their _____ activities.
   a. help—useful
   b. trouble—dynamic
   c. service—harmful

3. Fact and Fancy were so _____ that no one could _____ them.
   a. connected—separate
   b. necessary—use
   c. respected—want

4. If one is to understand the _____, one must study the _____.
   a. facts—unnecessary
   b. unusual—sentences
   c. whole—parts

5. His father _____ him, for he realized the interest was more than a _____ fancy.
   a. encouraged—childish
   b. berated—sincere
   c. helped—mature

6. Safe driving prevents _____ and the awful _____ of knowing you have caused an accident.
   a. disease—remainder
   b. accidents—safe
   c. tragedy—remorse

PAGE 31

Circle the word which best fits each sentence.

Saving your (1) _____ to eat at a later date is not always (2) _____. It may not wait as long as you do!
1. land   greed   luck   **dessert**
2. golden   **wise**   fair   sure

Many (3) _____ may indeed make for light work, but only if they work (4) _____.
3. **shovels**   seas   **hands**   kitchens
4. **together** alone   nearby   silently

"Put your money where your mouth is" may be a (5) _____-inflicting proverb; but it sure (6) _____ people quiet!
5. plant   **gold**   wise   **germ**
6. invests   **keeps**   shuts   tempts

Go ahead and rollerblade along life's (7) _____, but keep those knee pads (8) _____ for the bumps along the way.
7. **problems** **lanes**   lamps   deeds
8. **ready**   quick   dangerous   softly

Music may indeed (9) _____ a savage beast, but only if the (10) _____ has an instrument nearby.
9. shoot   ride   **calm**   scale
10. lion   trumpet   radio   **musician**

The saying "A fool and his money are soon (11) _____" should not be discussed when (12) _____ allowance off our folks.
11. **parted**   happy   peaceful   **shown**
12. sewing   waving   giving   **begging**

As Uncle Gene (13) _____ on his inflatable raft on the (14) _____, we knew that some men are islands!
13. flew   **fetched**   **floated**   fared
14. dock   **lake**   sink   house

Hurtling downward into a deep, dark (15) _____, Bernard exclaimed, "Why sure! Gotta (16) _____ before ya' leap!"
15. mansion   Chevy   **chasm**   rim
16. **look**   shave   care   buy

PAGE 32

Concept words are words that have to do with a certain **topic or subject**. Read the passage carefully.

Volcanoes!

Volcanoes are special kinds of mountains. Under volcanoes, deep in the earth, is a layer of hot, liquid rock called **magma**. Volcanoes are formed when the magma is suddenly forced up through a crack in the **crust**, or surface, of the earth. This action, called **eruption**, spills the hot magma, or lava, out onto the crust. As it cools, it hardens and forms mounds.

Scientists classify volcanoes in three groups. The first group includes volcanoes that have not erupted in hundreds of years. These volcanoes are **extinct** and are unlikely to erupt again. The second group also includes volcanoes that have not erupted in many years but these volcanoes are thought to be capable of erupting again. These volcanoes are called **dormant**. The final group includes volcanoes that erupted not long ago and could erupt again at any time. These volcanoes are said to be **active**.

Find and write a **boldfaced** word from the story for each description.

1. __magma__ liquid rock beneath the earth
2. __extinct__ group of volcanoes unlikely to erupt
3. __crust__ the outer surface of the earth
4. __eruption__ action that forces magma through the crust
5. __active__ group of volcanoes that have recently erupted
6. __dormant__ group of volcanoes that have not erupted in many years but still may erupt

PAGE 33

Fill in the blanks to show the scientific process of respiration.

water	work	carbon dioxide
energy	sugar	oxygen
cells	roots	

Plant cells take in __carbon dioxide__ and __sugar__.
Tubes carry these from the leaves to the __roots__ and other parts of the plant. The other plant parts use the carbon dioxide to break the sugar down into __water__ and __oxygen__ which release __energy__. The __cells__ will use this energy to do __work__.

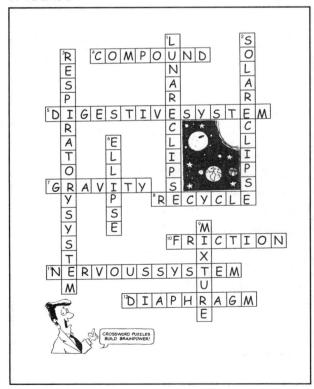

PAGE 34

Use the clues to complete the crossword puzzle on page 35.

Across

4. a substance that is formed when two elements chemically combine
5. a system that changes food into a form that cells can use
7. the force that pulls heavenly bodies toward each other
8. to use something over again
10. the force that resists motion between two objects in contact
11. a system that consists of the brain, spinal cord, and nerve fibers
12. a large muscle that helps you breathe

Down

1. an eclipse in which the moon moves through Earth's shadow
2. an eclipse in which the moon's shadow falls upon the Earth
3. a system that brings air into and out of the body
6. the shape of all the planets' orbits around the sun
9. two or more substances that are mixed together but not chemically combined

nervous system	friction	recycle
compound	diaphragm	gravity
digestive system	solar eclipse	mixture
respiratory system	lunar eclipse	ellipse

PAGE 35

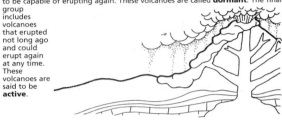

PAGE 36

Read the passage carefully. Use each of the **boldfaced** words in a sentence below.

Hundreds of years ago, people believed in a **variety** of **mythical**, or imaginary, creatures. Two **legendary** characters from myths were the unnatural, strange-looking, grotesque creatures called **gargoyles**, and the **Cyclops**, a giant with one eye.

One of the most **attractive**, or likable, of mythical beasts was the sleek, one-horned, **unicorn**. Another famous animal was the flying horse, **Pegasus**. He had wings that carried him high into the sky.

Have you read about any of these **fantastic**, or strange, creatures?

1. The ___legendary___ characters came from myths or legends passed down through hundreds of years.

2. Grotesque, unnatural figures were known as ___gargoyles___.

3. ___Pegasus___ was a famous winged horse.

4. A mythical giant with one eye in the middle of its forehead was known as ___Cyclops___.

5. A ___mythical___ creature isn't real. It's imaginary.

6. A number of different kinds of things are a ___variety___.

7. The unicorn, an ___attractive___ animal, was pleasing and likable.

8. The old, wild, or strange creatures seem ___fantastic___ to us.

9. The ___unicorn___, a mythical beast with one horn, is my favorite.

PAGE 37

Read the passage carefully.

Computer Data

Computers may seem "smart" but they cannot think. The only thing they can do is follow a set of instructions called a **program** which must be written by a person. The computer **hardware** (machinery) and **software** (programs) work together.

For the computer to work, a person must enter **data**, or information, into the computer. This is called **input**. New data is entered by typing on a **keyboard** that has letters and symbols like a typewriter. Data may be stored on a **disk** which is used to record and save information.

Next, the computer "reads" the data and follows the instructions of the program. The program may tell it to organize the data, compare it to other data, or store it for later use. This is called data **processing**.

When the processing is complete, the computer can display the results either on the screen or printed on paper as a **printout**.

Find and write a **boldfaced** word from the passage for each description.

1. ___disk___ used to save and record information
2. ___processing___ organizing, comparing, or storing data
3. ___program___ results printed on paper
4. ___data___ set of instructions for a computer
5. ___hardware___ computer machinery
6. ___input___ entering data
7. ___software___ computer programs
8. ___keyboard___ used for typing in data

PAGE 38

Sensory words describe something you **see, hear, smell, touch,** or **taste**. Choose a word from the word box that describes each phrase.

steamy	bitter
murmur	deafening
coarse	smooth
dim	fragrant
rustling	screeching

1. grasping steel wool ___coarse___
2. a crowd of people yelling ___deafening___
3. marble surface ___smooth___
4. blooming roses ___fragrant___
5. unsweetened chocolate ___bitter___
6. leaves in the wind ___rustling___
7. sitting in a sauna ___steamy___
8. an owl in the night ___screeching___

PAGE 39

Match the sense with the sensory word.

see — murmur
touch — dim
hear — bitter
smell — smooth
taste — salty

Write a sentence using each of the sensory words above.

1. _____
2. _____
3. _____
4. _____
5. _____

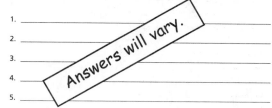
Answers will vary.

PAGE 40

Rewrite each sentence with at least two sensory words.

1. This is my sister.

   Answers may vary.

2. Have you seen my fish?

   Answers may vary.

3. I am sad today.

   Answers may vary.

4. That movie is good.

   Answers may vary.

5. I saw an animal.

   Answers may vary.

PAGE 41

Onomatopoeia is a word that **sounds like the sound** it describes, such as **snap, pop,** and **swish.** Write a poem describing a thunderstorm, the ocean, or an April rain shower using onomatopoeia words.

Answers will vary.

PAGE 42

Read the onomatopoeia words. Write a sentence using each word.

1. crunch

2. hum

3. zonk

4. sigh

5. snap

6. clatter

Answers will vary.

PAGE 43

A **plural** word is **more than one** of a person, place, or thing. Remember to add **es** to words that end in **x, sh,** and **ch,** to change **y** to **i** and add **es,** and to change **f** to **v** and add **es.** Change each word to the plural form. Write it on the line.

1. The ___squirrels___ are hiding in the ___ditches___ .
     squirrel   ditch

2. You will see ___seals___ at many ___beaches___ .
                    seal   beach

3. Put the ___fireflies___ in the ___jars___ .
              firefly   jar

4. How many ___berries___ did you pick from the ___bushes___ ?
                berry   bush

5. Put the ___letters___ in the ___mailboxes___ .
             letter   mailbox

6. Put the ___brushes___ on the ___shelves___ .
             brush   shelf

7. I bought two ___watches___ for my ___friends___ .
                  watch   friend

8. We saw ten ___birds___ on three ___branches___ .
                bird   branch

9. I want two ___lollipops___ for my ___sisters___ .
               lollipop   sister

10. The ___babies___ are taking their ___naps___ .
            baby   nap

PAGE 44

Make each word plural and write it in the correct column.

Hint: If there's a vowel before the **y**, add **s**.
If there's a consonant, change the **y** to **i** and add **es**.

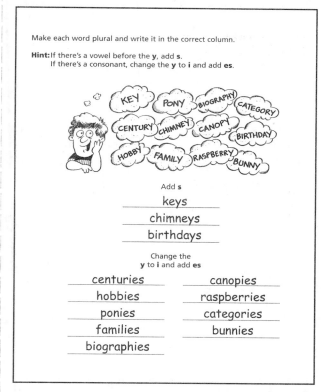

Add **s**

keys

chimneys

birthdays

Change the
y to **i** and add **es**

centuries	canopies
hobbies	raspberries
ponies	categories
families	bunnies
biographies	

PAGE 45

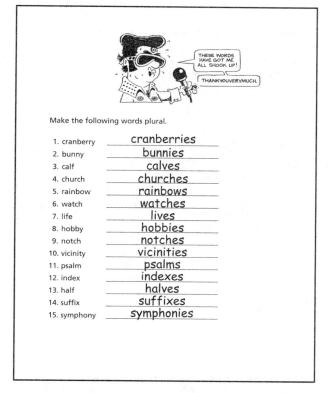

Make the following words plural.

1.	cranberry	cranberries
2.	bunny	bunnies
3.	calf	calves
4.	church	churches
5.	rainbow	rainbows
6.	watch	watches
7.	life	lives
8.	hobby	hobbies
9.	notch	notches
10.	vicinity	vicinities
11.	psalm	psalms
12.	index	indexes
13.	half	halves
14.	suffix	suffixes
15.	symphony	symphonies

PAGE 46

Write the plural of each word in the line. Then write the plural in the correct box puzzle.

1.	match	matches	9.	calf	calves
2.	city	cities	10.	penny	pennies
3.	school	schools	11.	child	children
4.	foot	feet	12.	piano	pianos
5.	body	bodies	13.	woman	women
6.	church	churches	14.	story	stories
7.	man	men	15.	sandwich	sandwiches
8.	radio	radios	16.	mouse	mice

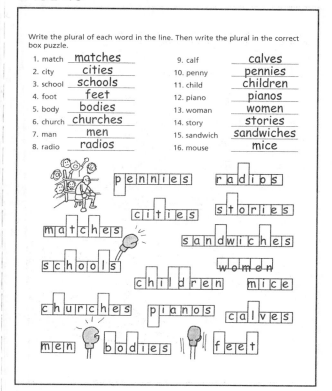

PAGE 47

A **suffix** is a word part added to the **end of a word** that changes its meaning. Use the suffix definitions in the box to write a definition of each word below.

> **ist** means "one who practices"
> **ous** means "full of"
> **ance** means "the state of"

1.	artist	one who makes art
2.	courageous	full of courage
3.	admittance	the state of admitting
4.	appearance	the state of appearing
5.	guitarist	one who practices guitar
6.	humorous	full of humor
7.	inheritance	the state of inheriting
8.	mountainous	full of mountains
9.	poisonous	full of poison
10.	violinist	one who practices the violin

PAGE 48

Add the suffix **ful** or **ly** to the word from the box that makes sense in the sentence.

harm	easy
care	glad
use	brave
rest	sudden
hope	clear

1. Please be __careful__ when you use the iron.
2. __Suddenly__ a flock of geese swept across the sky.
3. Our vacation at the beach was so __restful__.
4. Sandy got an A on her speech because she spoke so __clearly__.
5. Our team is __hopeful__ that we will make the playoffs.
6. Some activities are __harmful__ to your health.
7. Manuel __bravely__ climbed the tree to get his sister's escaped parakeet.
8. I will __gladly__ deliver your papers for you while you are gone.
9. Your notes will be __useful__ as you prepare for the test.
10. The class aced the test __easily__.

PAGE 49

Add the suffix **less** or **ness** to complete each sentence.

1. We adopted a home __less__ dog from the pound.
2. My favorite thing about the dog is the soft __ness__ of its fur.
3. The thick __ness__ of its fur keeps the dog warm.
4. Dark __ness__ scared our dog at first, so it slept in my brother's room.
5. It was use __less__ to try to break the dog of that habit!
6. Our house was never spot __less__ before the dog arrived, but it is definitely messy now.
7. Feeling at home with our new pet was pain __less__.
8. We were not care __less__ when we named our dog.

PAGE 50

Write the word with a suffix from the word box that fits the definition.

supportive	patience
absence	intelligence
truthful	forgetful
thoughtful	doubtful
cheerful	active

1. thinking carefully __thoughtful__
2. has trouble remembering __forgetful__
3. having a sunny attitude __cheerful__
4. keeping busy __active__
5. disbelieving or questioning __doubtful__
6. always telling the truth __truthful__
7. the state of not being present __absence__
8. smartness __intelligence__
9. showing great care or concern __supportive__
10. ability to wait calmly __patience__

PAGE 51

Write the definition of each word using the suffix definitions in the word box.

ness	quality of being
ble	capable of being

1. bleak<u>ness</u> __quality of being bleak__
2. permiss<u>ible</u> __capable of being permitted__
3. break<u>able</u> __capable of being broken__
4. blind<u>ness</u> __quality of being blind__
5. steadi<u>ness</u> __quality of being steady__
6. admiss<u>ible</u> __capable of being admitted__
7. furri<u>ness</u> __quality of being furry__
8. believ<u>able</u> __capable of being believed__

PAGE 52

Complete each sentence using a word with a suffix from the word box.

collection	invitation
capable	improvements
peaceful	addition
wonderful	marvelous

1. My birthday was __wonderful__ .

2. This is my __collection__ of stamps.

3. It is so __peaceful__ up in the mountains.

4. In __addition__ to dance lessons, I take piano and clarinet.

5. The __invitation__ for the wedding came yesterday.

6. The movie was __marvelous__ !

7. Dad is working on a few home __improvements__ .

8. He is not __capable__ of lifting all those heavy boxes himself.

PAGE 53

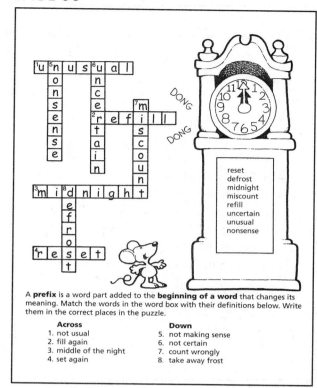

DONG DONG

reset
defrost
midnight
miscount
refill
uncertain
unusual
nonsense

A **prefix** is a word part added to the **beginning of a word** that changes its meaning. Match the words in the word box with their definitions below. Write them in the correct places in the puzzle.

Across
1. not usual
2. fill again
3. middle of the night
4. set again

Down
5. not making sense
6. not certain
7. count wrongly
8. take away frost

PAGE 54

Match each word with its meaning. Write the number of the word by its meaning.

1. exhale   __2__ breathe in
2. inhale   __1__ breathe out

3. misread   __3__ read wrongly
4. reread   __4__ read again

5. bicycle   __5__ three-wheeled cycle
6. tricycle   __6__ two-wheeled cycle

Use the words above to complete the sentences.

1. Allen likes to __inhale__ the fresh mountain air.

2. Carmen is in a __bicycle__ race today.

3. The model airplane you put together may not work if you __misread__ the directions.

4. The baby's __tricycle__ is in the garage.

5. Matt wants to __reread__ this book.

6. Take in a deep breath, then __exhale__ .

PAGE 55

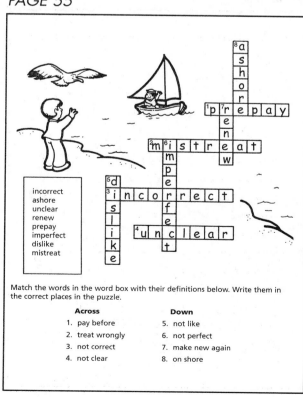

incorrect
ashore
unclear
renew
prepay
imperfect
dislike
mistreat

Match the words in the word box with their definitions below. Write them in the correct places in the puzzle.

Across
1. pay before
2. treat wrongly
3. not correct
4. not clear

Down
5. not like
6. not perfect
7. make new again
8. on shore

PAGE 56

Match each word with its meaning. Write the number of the word by its meaning.

1. increase   **1** become larger
2. decrease   **2** become smaller

3. indirect   **4** direct again
4. redirect   **3** not direct

5. inflate   **6** to let out air
6. deflate   **5** to blow air into

Use the words above to complete the sentences.

1. When I **deflate** the tire, it will be flat.
2. To make more soup, **increase** the amount of water.
3. Nick took an **indirect** route to school.
4. If you are lost, a police officer can **redirect** you.
5. Here are twenty balloons to **inflate** for the party.
6. The price of shirts will **decrease** during the big sale.

PAGE 57

Complete each sentence with a **con** word from the word box.

converged	controversy	contorted	conclude	consult
convince	conduct	conscious	congested	confetti
contrition	contestant	conservation	conjured	

1. The mall was **congested** with swarms of sale-crazed customers.
2. Did you **convince** your teacher that they are a good group?
3. Please **consult** your doctor if your fever continues.
4. Peter's face **contorted** in pain as his horse stomped on his foot.
5. The two highways **converged** before we reached Toronto.
6. Our **conservation** group hopes to plant 50 trees this Saturday.
7. The tearful toddler, filled with **contrition**, told her dead goldfish that she only meant to take it for a walk.
8. Are you **conscious**, Henry? Speak to me if you can hear me!
9. The brawny guide will **conduct** us to the bottom of the gorge.
10. Our meeting will **conclude** in twenty minutes.
11. There was a horrid **controversy** about the music selection chosen for the skating party.
12. What evil the wicked warlock **conjures** against his unsuspecting apprentice!
13. When the first **contestant** could not answer the riddle, he was sentenced to nine years hard dishwashing.
14. After our team won, we tossed **confetti** high into the air to celebrate.

PAGE 58

Read the story. Use the prefixes in the word box to write in the missing prefixes.

un	tele	dis	re	mis

Star Trip

As usual, the Little Prince of Mars sat in front of his big-screen **tele**vision. "This life is very **un**interesting," he thought. Just then, he heard a knock at the door. When he opened the door, a messenger handed him a **tele**gram. "There must be some **mis**take," said the Little Prince. But when he opened the envelope, he was surprised. The **un**happy frown on his face **dis**appeared. He was going on a trip to the stars! The Little Prince was **un**certain what to pack. He dashed for his **tele**scope and magic crystal kit. He packed and **re**packed his star travel bag until everything fit. Someday he would **re**turn to his own planet, but until then, he was ready for an adventure in the stars!

PAGE 59

Many words consist of one or more **Greek** or **Latin root**. For example, the Greek root **tele** means far. When it is combined with **vis**, the Latin root for **see**, we get **television**. Fill in the blanks below to learn the meaning of more roots.

1. Telephones allow us to hear sounds from far away. **Tele** means **far**, and **phone** comes from the Greek word meaning **ground**.
2. **Ped** is a root word meaning foot. Therefore, a **pedestrian** is a person who travels by **foot**.
3. **Graph** comes from the Greek word meaning to write, and **auto** is the root word for self. Thus, an **autograph** is **your signature**.
4. **Geo** is the Greek root for Earth. **Geography**, then, is writing or drawing about the **Earth**.
5. **Bio** is the root word meaning life. When someone writes an **autobiography**, he or she writes about **their own life**.
6. A **biographer** writes about **someone else's life**.
7. The word **pedometer** combines the root **ped** with **meter**, a root meaning measurement. A **pedometer** is an instrument for **measuring** the distance someone travels by **foot**.
8. **Logy** is a Greek root for study. When combined with the root **graph**, we get **graphology** or the study of **writing**.
9. **Biology** is the study of **life**.
10. **Geology** is the study of **Earth**.
11. Writing that comes from far away is called a **telegraph**.
12. Combine the root word for sound and the root for write. The machine we use to play records is a **phonograph**.

PAGE 60

Add new words to your vocabulary by understanding these Greek or Latin roots.

1. **Magna** or **magni** is the Latin root for great. **Magnificent** is an adjective that means excellent or great.
2. **Aqua** is the Latin word meaning water. An **aquarium** is a place for keeping water plants and **aquatic** animals.
3. **Flor** is the Latin root for flower. A **florist** sells or grows flowers for a living.
4. **Dict** is the Latin root meaning to speak. **Diction** means the manner in which words are spoken.
5. **Micro** comes from the Greek word *mikros*, meaning tiny or small. A **microscope** is an instrument that allows us to see very small things.

Use a dictionary to find two words formed from each of the above roots. Write words and their definitions in the blanks below.

root	dictionary word	definition
1. **magna** or **magni**	(a) _____	(a) _____
	(b) _____	(b) _____
2. **aqua**	(a) _____	(a) _____
	(b) _____	(b) _____
3. **flor**	(a) _____	(a) _____
	(b) _____	(b) _____
4. **dict**	(a) _____	(a) _____
	(b) _____	(b) _____
5. **micro**	(a) _____	(a) _____
	(b) _____	(b) _____

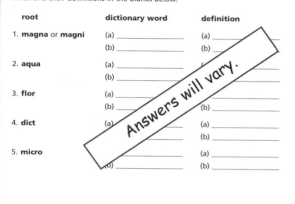

Answers will vary.

PAGE 61

aqua, aque	water
aqualung	breathing equipment for underwater swimming or diving
aquamarine	a bluish sea-green color
aquaplane	a wide board that is towed by a motorboat, like a single water ski
aquarium	an artificial pond or tank of water where live water animals and water plants are kept; a building where such collections are exhibited
aquatic	growing or living in water
aqueduct	a channel that carries large amounts of water

Divide the following words into parts so that **aqua (or aque)** is separate.

Example: aqua   rium

1. aquamarine   aqua   marine
2. aqualung   aqua   lung
3. aquaplane   aqua   plane
4. aqueduct   aque   duct

Complete each sentence using a word from the word box.

1. To go scuba diving, you need to wear an **aqualung**.
2. The children bought a variety of fish for the **aquarium**.
3. Seaweed is an **aquatic** plant.
4. The Romans used an **aqueduct** to transport water from one place to another.
5. Susan liked to waterski, but her brother John preferred to use an **aquaplane**.

PAGE 62

dict	to say
dictate	to say something aloud that will be written or recorded by another; to command or order
dictator	a ruler with unlimited power
diction	a style of speaking; the degree of preciseness or clarity in speech
predict	to foretell or say ahead of time that something will happen
verdict	a judgment or decision, especially that of a jury in a court case

Circle the root that means **to say** in the following words.

1. **dic**tion
2. pre**dict**
3. **dic**tator
4. ver**dict**

Complete each sentence using a word from the word box.

1. The foreman of the jury announced the **verdict**: not guilty.
2. The actor was very careful of his **diction** during the audition.
3. The manager will **dictate** the new rules to the employees.
4. I **predict** that my little brother will have a dent in his new bike before the end of the week.

PAGE 63

spec	to see, to look at
aspect	the look or appearance of anything
introspective	examining one's own thoughts and feelings
specimen	a single part or thing used as a sample or example of a whole group
spectacle	anything viewed or seen; a public performance
spectator	a person who watches an event
spectrum	the range of colors visible to the human eye; a continuous range or entire extent

Unscramble these words. Write the correct word next to its meaning.

calcepest   casttrope   pacset   victorinestep   mesnepic

1. the way a person or a thing looks   **aspect**
2. a typical part or example   **specimen**
3. looking into one's own mind and feelings   **introspective**
4. something to look at   **spectacle**
5. an onlooker   **spectator**

Complete each sentence using a word from the word box.

1. The circus advertised itself as the greatest **spectacle** in the world.
2. No one realized he was ever **introspective**, because he always seemed so self-confident.
3. The investigator asked for a **specimen** of everyone's handwriting.
4. You can find the whole **spectrum** of types in our school—from preppie to punk.
5. In bruising games like football and soccer, I'd rather be a **spectator** than a participant.
6. Elsie's whole **aspect** reflected what an absolutely terrible week it had been.

Answer the questions below.

What is a spectator sport? **A sport where people watch.**

List four spectator sports. **Answers will vary.**

PAGE 64

	deca, deci	ten, tenth
decade	a period of ten years	
decathlon	an athletic contest in which each contestant participates in ten events	
decibel	a unit of sound intensity	
decimal	a fraction with an unwritten denominator of ten, indicated by a decimal point before the numerator	
decimate	to kill or destroy a large part of (originally, to kill every tenth person)	

Fill in each blank with a word from the word box.

1. In the Middle Ages, the Black Plague __decimated__ (ed) the population of Europe.
2. To win a __decathlon__, you must excel at ten different sports.
3. The __decibel__ level of the jackhammer hurt my ears.
4. Rhonda can recite the numerical value of pi to the tenth __decimal__.
5. My uncle is 50, so he has lived through five __decades__ (s).

Answer the questions below.

1. Name five important events in the first decade of your life.

   __Answers will vary.__

2. Use an encyclopedia or an almanac to compare the decibel levels of a whisper, a jet plane, and rock music. At what level is sound considered painful?

   __Answers will vary.__

PAGE 65

	circ, circum	around, circle
circa	about or approximately	
circuitous	roundabout; indirect; devious	
circulation	the act of moving in a circle or circuit or of moving from place to place	
circumference	the outer line of a circle; the length of this line	
circumnavigate	to sail around something, especially the world	
circumscribe	to draw or form a line around, especially a circle; to limit or restrain	
circumspect	careful to consider all related circumstances before acting or deciding; cautious	
circumvent	to avoid or find a way around	

Look up the following words in a dictionary. Briefly define each word in the blank that follows it.

1. circadian — 24 hour cycles
2. circuitry — electronic circuits
3. circumflex — to bend around
4. circumstantial — incidental

Fill in each blank with a word from the word box.

1. Johnny came up with some very creative excuses to __circumvent__ doing his homework.
2. Ferdinand Magellan's ship was the first to __circumnavigate__ the world.
3. On her first day at the new school, Marie was __circumspect__; she wanted to get a sense of the various crowds before she picked new friends.
4. When his parents said he could never stay out past nine o'clock, Arthur felt he was being unreasonably __circumscribed__ (d).
5. The doctor said that my grandmother must find some type of exercise that would help improve the __circulation__ of her blood.

PAGE 66

	ject	to throw
abject	contemptible; humble; wretched	
conjecture	a guess or a judgment without sufficient evidence	
dejected	sad and depressed	
eject	to force out or cause to be removed	
interject	to break in with a comment while someone else is speaking	
projectile	something thrown or fired through the air	
rejection	a refusal to accept or to use	
trajectory	the path, especially a curve, traced by a moving object	

Fill in each blank with a word from the word box.

1. The tornado turned trees and shingles into dangerous __projectile__ (s).
2. He offered an __dejected__ apology.
3. Just before the plane crashed, the pilot pushed the button that would __eject__ him.
4. The crowd followed the __trajectory__ of the ball as it sailed out of the ballpark.
5. His accusation was based only on __conjecture__.
6. "I know the answer," she __interjected__ (ed) before the game-show emcee could even finish asking the question.

Circle the root that means **to throw**. Write a sentence using each word.

1. project (noun)
2. adjective
3. injection
4. reject (noun)
5. interjection
6. object (noun)
7. subject (noun)

__Answers will vary.__

PAGE 67

An **imported word** is an English word that **comes from another language**.

PARLEZ VOUZ FRANÇAIS?

catalogue	carrousel	boulevard	question
bouquet	budget	crayon	menu
lieu	bandage	rare	cinema

Complete each sentence with a French word from the word box.

1. Let's use the skateboard in __lieu__ of the skates.
2. Do you want to ask me a __question__?
3. I think I need a __bandage__ for this cut.
4. Let's ride our bikes down the __boulevard__.
5. Riding the horses on the __carrousel__ was great!
6. That is a beautiful __bouquet__ of flowers!
7. What movies are playing at the __cinema__ today?
8. Do you have a magenta __crayon__ I can use?
9. Before we decide what to order, let's study the __menu__.
10. I want to look at the __catalogue__ before I decide what clothes to buy.
11. Sticking to a __budget__ keeps you from spending too much.
12. That albino snake is very __rare__.

PAGE 68

Throughout history, English-speaking people have borrowed words from other languages. Many dictionaries give an **etymology** or short word history to tell the origin of a word.

Look up the following list of words in a dictionary. Write the definition beside the word.

1. **comrade** (from Spanish) _companion or friend_
2. **caravan** (from Persian) _a group of travelers_
3. **bungalow** (from Hindi) _a cottage of one story_
4. **scant** (from Danish) _barely sufficient in amount_
5. **solo** (from Italian) _any performance by one person_
6. **clan** (from Gaelic) _a group of families_

Use the words from above to complete the following sentences.

7. My grandparents live in a new _bungalow_ near the mountains.
8. The _scant_ rations were not enough to feed the campers.
9. The girl will sing a _solo_ at the talent show.
10. The hiker helped his _comrade_ climb up the steep slope.
11. The four families are all members of the same _clan_ in Scotland.
12. The truck drivers formed a _caravan_ for the long drive through the desert.

PAGE 69

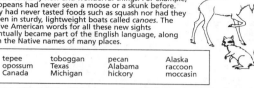

Native Americans introduced European explorers and settlers to many new and wonderful things. For example, Europeans had never seen a moose or a skunk before. They had never tasted foods such as squash nor had they ridden in sturdy, lightweight boats called *canoes*. The Native American words for all these new sights eventually became part of the English language, along with the Native names of many places.

tepee	toboggan	pecan	Alaska
opossum	Texas	Alabama	raccoon
Canada	Michigan	hickory	moccasin

Below is a list of Native American words and their meanings. Write the English words from the word box beside the corresponding Native American term.

Native American Word	Meaning	English Word
1. tejas	friends, allies	Texas
2. kanata	village	Canada
3. aposoum	white animal	opossum
4. alayeska	great land	Alaska
5. pacane	hard-shelled nut	pecan
6. michigama	great lake	Michigan
7. topagan	drag made of skin	toboggan
8. aroughcun	scratcher	raccoon
9. pocahiquara	food made from pounded nuts	hickory
10. mokkussin	shoe	moccasin
11. alibamu	I clear the thicket	Alabama
12. tipi	ti — to dwell pi — to use for	tepee

PAGE 70

January was named for Janus, the Roman god of doors, who had a face that looked to the past and one that looked to the future.

February came from the Latin word *februare*, which means *to purify*. During this month, the Romans purified themselves for festivals.

March was named for Mars, the Roman god of war.

April may have gotten its name from the Latin word *aperire*, which means *to open*, or from Aphrodite, the Greek goddess of love.

May was named for Maia, the Roman goddess of spring.

June is thought to have been named for Juno, the Roman goddess of marriage.

July was named in honor of Julius Caesar, a Roman statesman born in this month.

August was named in honor of the Roman emperor Augustus.

September came from the Latin word *septem*, which means *seven*. In the old Roman calendar, September was the seventh month.

October came from the Latin word *octo* for *eight*. October was once the eighth month.

November came from the Latin word *novem*, which means *nine*. In the old Roman calendar, November was the ninth month.

December was named after the Latin word *decem*, which means *ten*. In the old Roman calendar, December was the tenth month.

Complete the puzzle using the words and their definitions in the word box.

Across
2. Named for Juno
5. Goddess of Spring
7. Comes from a Latin word meaning *nine*
9. Latin word for *seven*
11. Caesar, a Roman statesman

Down
1. Meaning of decem
2. God of doors
3. A month for purifying
4. Named for goddess of love
6. Named for a Roman emperor
8. Latin word for *eight*
10. God of war

PAGE 71

Read the chart to find out where the names for the days of the week came from.

Modern English	Old English	Meaning	
Sunday	Sunnandaeg	*day of the sun*	Named in honor of the sun
Monday	Monandaeg	*day of the moon*	Named in honor of the moon
Tuesday	Tiwesdaeg	*Tyr's day*	Named after Tyr, the norse god of war
Wednesday	Wodnesdaeg	*Woden's day*	Named after Woden, the chief god in Norse mythology
Thursday	Thuresdaeg	*Thor's day*	Named after Thor, the Norse god of thunder
Friday	Frigedaeg	*Frigg's day*	Named after Frigg, the Norse goddess of love and Woden's wife
Saturday	Saeter-daeg	*Saturn's day*	Named after Saturn, the Roman god of agriculture

Write the days of the week in Modern English.

1. Thuresdaeg _Thursday_   5. Monandaeg _Monday_
2. Wodnesdaeg _Wednesday_   6. Frigedaeg _Friday_
3. Sunnandaeg _Sunday_   7. Tiwesdaeg _Tuesday_
4. Saeter-daeg _Saturday_

Answer the questions. Use the Old English term for the days of the week.

8. What day is today? _____
9. What day is tomorrow? _____
10. What day is the last day of this month? _____
11. On what day does your birthday fall this year? _____
12. On what day do you stay up the latest? _____

Answers will vary.

PAGE 72

The myths of the ancient Greeks and Romans were filled with powerful gods and goddesses. The names of these supernatural beings became the sources of many English words.

Write the name of the Greek god or goddess who inspired each of the words below.

Ceres —	Roman goddess of the harvest
Gaea —	Greek goddess of the earth
Hypnos —	Greek god of sleep
Jove —	another name for Jupiter, king of the gods in Roman mythology
Muses —	Greek goddesses of art and science
Pan —	Greek god of the woods who was able to fill people with sudden terror
Titans —	a family of giants in Greek mythology

1. **cereal**—different types of grain
   Ceres
2. **geology**—the study of the history of the earth
   Gaea
3. **museum**—a place where works of art are displayed
   Muses
4. **hypnosis**—a method of putting people in a state that resembles sleep
   Hypnos
5. **panic**—a feeling of strong, uncontrollable fear _Pan_
6. **jovial**—jolly, happy _Nove_
7. **titanic**—huge, powerful _Titans_

Fill in the blanks with the **boldfaced** words above.

8. We saw a colorful painting at the _museum_.
9. Our class studied _geology_ and learned about how different types of rocks formed.
10. A person under _hypnosis_ sometimes looks asleep.
11. What kind of _cereal_ do you enjoy for breakfast?
12. My Aunt Julie is so _jovial_ that we call her Aunt Jolly.
13. _titanic_ The wave that swept the shore during last year's storm was _____!
14. It is important not to _panic_ when you are in danger.

PAGE 73

Abbreviations are **the shortened version** of a word.

Rewrite Yuki's birthday invitation using abbreviations.

What: Yuki's Eleventh Birthday Party
Yuki's 11th Birthday Party

When: Saturday, January Tenth
Sat., Jan. 10th

Where: Seven Hundred Eighty Six Maple Boulevard
786 Maple Blvd.

Rewrite the directions to Yuki's house without the abbreviations.

1. Take MLK Jr. Hwy to Rt. 7. Turn rt.
   Take Martin Luther King Junior Highway to Route Seven. Turn right.
2. Go 4 mi. to 1st light. Turn rt.
   Go four miles to the first light. Turn right.
3. Maple Blvd. is the 2nd St. on the lt.
   Maple Boulevard is the second street on the left.
4. 786 is the 3rd house on the rt.
   Seven hundred eighty six is the third house on the right.

PAGE 74

Rewrite Isabel's planner entries without abbreviations. Check the word box for help with abbreviations you don't know.

cash on	building
delivery	meeting
appointment	dozen

1. Dentist appt. Sat. Feb. 2
   Dentist appointment Saturday February 2
2. soccer booster mtg. Mon. after school
   soccer booster meeting Monday after school
3. Fri. May 6 camping trip—meet at Bldg.2
   Friday May 6 camping trip—meet at Building 2
4. 1st soccer game Tues. Apr 11
   First soccer game Tuesday April 11
5. pick up doz. roses for Mother's Day May 13.
   pick up dozen roses for Mother's Day May 13
6. deliver fund raiser candy, c.o.d.
   deliver fund raiser candy, cash on delivery

PAGE 75

Rewrite each statement without abbreviations.

Celsius	millimeter
inch	pound
yard	centimeter
ounces	mile
foot	dozen
Fahrenheit	

1. 3 ft. make 1 yd.
   3 feet make a yard
2. 12 in. make 1 ft.
   12 inches make 1 foot
3. there are 16 oz. in 1 lb.
   there are 16 ounces in 1 pound
4. 1 doz. is made of 12 objects
   1 dozen is made of 12 objects
5. there are 5280 ft. in 1 mi.
   there are 5280 feet in 1 mile
6. there are 1760 yd. in 1 mi.
   there are 1760 yards in 1 mile
7. there are 100 mm in 1 cm
   there are 100 millimeters in 1 centimeter
8. 32 degrees F is equal to 0 degrees C
   32 degrees fahrenheit is equal to 0 degrees Celsius

PAGE 76

Match each abbreviation to its meaning.

1. Rd.	E	A.	ante meridiem (before noon)
2. B.C.	J	B.	parkway
3. A.D.	M	C.	post office
4. A.M.	A	D.	rural route or railroad
5. P.M.	H	E.	road
6. St.	L	F.	avenue
7. Pkwy.	B	G.	drive or doctor
8. S.E.	S	H.	post meridiem (after noon)
9. Ln.	K	I.	mount or mountain
10. R.R.	D	J.	before Christ
11. Mt.	I	K.	lane
12. P.O.	C	L.	street
13. Ave.	F	M.	anno Domini (in the year of the Lord)
14. Blvd.	T	N.	miles per hour
15. m.p.h.	N	O.	northeast
16. N.W.	R	P.	southwest
17. S.W.	P	Q.	miles per gallon
18. N.E.	O	R.	northwest
19. Dr.	G	S.	southeast
20. m.p.g.	Q	T.	boulevard

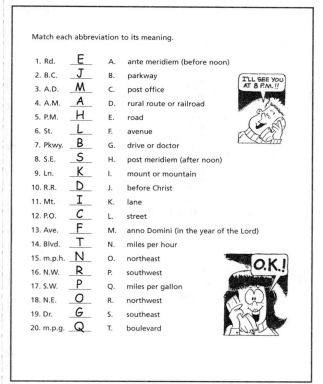

PAGE 77

A **compound word** combines **two words to make a new word.**

Write a word from the bubbles on each line to form a compound word.

1. camp — fire
2. candle — stick
3. honey — comb
4. dream — land
5. knap — sack
6. drift — wood
7. thanks — giving
8. mountain — top
9. pop — corn
10. water — melon
11. wind — storm
12. trail — blazer
13. soap — suds
14. glass — blower
15. fish — hook
16. tooth — paste

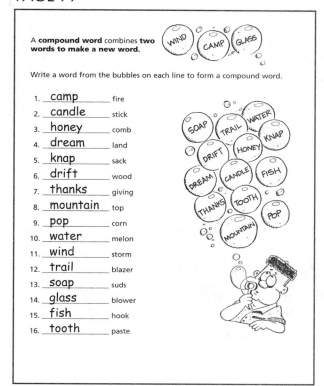

PAGE 78

Write a sentence for each compound word you formed on page 77.

1.
2.
3.
4.
5.
6.
7.
8.
9.
10.
11.
12.
13.
14.
15.
16.

Answers will vary.

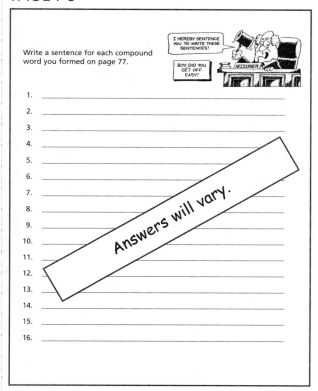

PAGE 79

Look at each picture clue below. Write the compound word it represents.

1. butterfly
2. honeycomb
3. horseshoe
4. quarterback
5. skateboard
6. homework
7. toadstool
8. turtleneck

PAGE 80

Combine the first number from Set A with the second number from Set B to make a compound word.

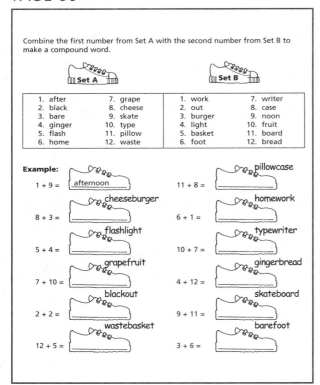

Set A

1. after	7. grape
2. black	8. cheese
3. bare	9. skate
4. ginger	10. type
5. flash	11. pillow
6. home	12. waste

Set B

1. work	7. writer
2. out	8. case
3. burger	9. noon
4. light	10. fruit
5. basket	11. board
6. foot	12. bread

Example:

1 + 9 = afternoon

8 + 3 = cheeseburger

5 + 4 = flashlight

7 + 10 = grapefruit

2 + 2 = blackout

12 + 5 = wastebasket

11 + 8 = pillowcase

6 + 1 = homework

10 + 7 = typewriter

4 + 12 = gingerbread

9 + 11 = skateboard

3 + 6 = barefoot

PAGE 81

Choose a word from the list on the right to combine with a word on the left to form a compound word.

Example:

M	1. chalk	chalkboard	a. piece
e	2. over	overdue	b. foot
r	3. tooth	toothache	c. cycle
i	4. apple	applesauce	d. mint
p	5. post	postmark	e. due
b	6. bare	barefoot	f. down
t	7. ear	earpick	g. spoon
a	8. mouth	mouthpiece	h. work
j	9. water	watermelon	i. sauce
g	10. table	tablespoon	j. melon
c	11. motor	motorcycle	k. right
s	12. wall	wallpaper	l. house
f	13. count	countdown	m. board
l	14. light	lighthouse	n. bread
d	15. pepper	peppermint	o. tub
q	16. basket	basketball	p. mark
n	17. ginger	gingerbread	q. ball
k	18. copy	copyright	r. ache
o	19. bath	bathtub	s. paper
h	20. home	homework	t. pick

PAGE 82

Use a word from word box 1 and a word from word box 2 to make a compound word for each meaning. Write the compound word.

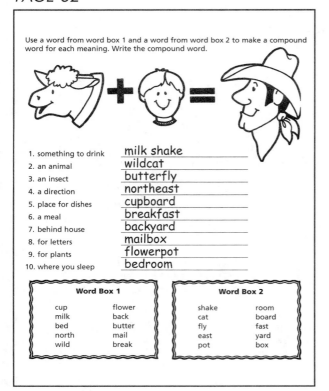

1. something to drink — milk shake
2. an animal — wildcat
3. an insect — butterfly
4. a direction — northeast
5. place for dishes — cupboard
6. a meal — breakfast
7. behind house — backyard
8. for letters — mailbox
9. for plants — flowerpot
10. where you sleep — bedroom

Word Box 1

cup	flower
milk	back
bed	butter
north	mail
wild	break

Word Box 2

shake	room
cat	board
fly	fast
east	yard
pot	box

Test-taking Practice is designed to prepare you to use the Vocabulary Skills you've been practicing in the first part of this book on a standardized test.

The first part of the Test-taking Practice is just for Vocabulary Skills. You'll answer questions that test your knowledge of synonyms, Antonyms, Homonyms, and Context Clues.

The second part of the Test-taking Practice is Reading Comprehension. On these pages, you will read a passage and then answer questions about it. The better your understanding of Vocabulary Skills, such as Context Clues, Concept Words, and Root and Base Words, the better you will do on Reading Comprehension, which indirectly tests these skills.

How to Use Test-Taking Practice

Getting Started:
- Read the directions carefully.
- Do the sample items.

Practice:
- Complete the Practice items.
- Continue working until you reach a Stop sign at the bottom of the page.

Sometime during school you may take a standardized achievement test. These tests check to see what you and the rest of your class have learned. they can help you see what your strengths and weaknesses are.

Taking a test can be stressful, but it doesn't have to be! The key is to prepare yourself, whether you are taking an achievement test or a weekly quiz. Here are some tips that can help you prepare for and do your best on any kind of test.

Before the test:
- Find a comfortable, quiet spot to study that is free of distractions.
- Get organized before you start to study: collect all the books, papers, notes, and pencils or pens you will need before you sit down.
- Study a little bit at a time, no more than 30 minutes a day. If you can, choose the same time each day to study in your quiet place. This is good practice for sitting and concentrating for the actual test.
- Give yourself frequent 5-minute breaks if you plan to study for longer than a half hour. Stand up, stretch out, and get a drink or snack (nothing too messy!)
- Try making a study sheet with all the information you think will be on the test. Have a parent, brother, sister, or friend quiz you by asking questions from the sheet.

On the day of the test:
- Get a good night's sleep before the test.
- Plan to eat a light breakfast and lunch so that you won't get drowsy during the test. Too much food can make you sleepy.
- Wear comfortable clothes that won't distract you during the test. If you have long hair, plan to pull it back away from your face so it won't distract you.
- Don't worry if you are a little nervous when you take a test. This is a natural feeling and may even help you stay alert.
- Take advantage of any breaks you have. Stand up and stretch, and get a drink of water or visit the bathroom if you have the time.

During the test:

Be careful

- Listen carefully to all the directions before you begin.
- Read all directions carefully.
- Sometimes the letters for the answer choices change for each question. Make sure the space you fill in matches the answer you think is correct.
- Read the question and all the answer choices. Once you have decided on the correct answer, ask yourself: "Does this really answer the question?"

Manage your time wisely

- Take the time to understand each question before you answer.
- Eliminate the answer choices that don't make sense.
- Try out answer choices in the question to see if they make sense.
- Skim through written passages and then read the questions. Refer back to the story to answer the questions. You don't have to reread the passage for each question.
- Look for key words in the question and the answer choices. They will help you find the correct answer.
- Sometimes the correct answer is not given. Mark "none" if this is the case.
- Skip difficult questions. Circle them and come back to them when you are finished with the easier questions.
- If there is still time when you have finished, go through the test again and check your answers.

Be confident

- Stay with your first answer. Change it only if you are certain another choice is better.
- Don't worry if you don't know an answer. Take your best guess if you are unsure of the answer, then move on to the next question.
- Be certain of what the question is asking before you answer. Try restating a question if you don't understand it the way it is written.

Examples   **Directions:** Read each item. Choose the word that means the same or about the same as the underlined word.

A a long **conflict**	B An **abrupt** stop is —
A friendship	F sudden
B time	G slow
C project	H planned
D struggle	J difficult

 **Look carefully at all the answer choices.**

When you mark your answer, be sure you are marking it in the right space in the answer rows.

Practice

1   carefully select

A eliminate
B measure
C choose
D align

2   circulate a rumor

F ignore
G hear
H trust
J spread

3   deeply eroded

A worn
B steep
C high
D rugged

4   pardon someone

F forgive
G slide
H pause
J compete

5   To irritate people is to —

A annoy
B chase
C enjoy
D visit

6   A forceful person is —

F weak
G foreign
H strong
J helpful

7   An insistent salesperson is —

A talented
B capable
C friendly
D persistent

8   A significant discovery is —

F profitable
G important
H unexpected
J surprising

Examples

Directions: Read each item. Choose the answer that means the same or about the same as the underlined word.

A Nothing but <u>nonsense</u>	**B** My sister felt <u>miserable</u> today.
A hopeless attitude	<u>Miserable</u> means —
B worthless money	**F** happy
C meaningless talk	**G** tired
D careless actions	**H** pleasant
	J terrible

 If a question is too difficult, skip it and come back to it later, if you have time.

Practice

1 Discuss the <u>situation</u>

    A length of time
    B state of affairs
    C recent news
    D type of weather

2 A <u>direct</u> answer

    F honest and truthful
    G dishonest and untruthful
    H correct
    J incorrect

3 <u>Approach</u> a town

    A recognize
    B live in
    C go away from
    D come near to

4 A successful <u>venture</u>

    F athletic competition
    G business
    H risky activity
    J career

5 Do you know if this is <u>edible</u>?

If something is <u>edible</u> it —

    A is fresh
    B has been damaged
    C tastes bitter
    D can be eaten

6 Janelle is <u>popular</u> at school.

<u>Popular</u> means —

    F liked by others
    G new
    H often late
    J unknown to others

7 The bus was late <u>again</u> today.

<u>Again</u> means —

    A for the first time
    B for the last time
    C more than once
    D a little bit

Examples

Directions: Read each item. Choose the answer that means the opposite of the underlined word.

A will <u>decline</u>	**B** <u>peddle</u> newspapers
A decrease	F read
B enlist	G buy
C increase	H sell
D pause	J order

If you are not sure which answer is correct, take your best guess.

Eliminate answers that mean the same as the underlined word.

Practice

1 be <u>lenient</u>

  A easy
  B complex
  C strict
  D written

2 <u>nourish</u> plants

  F starve
  G cultivate
  H harvest
  J rescue

3 <u>rare</u> disease

  A unusual
  B severe
  C mild
  D common

4 try to <u>surrender</u>

  F follow
  G resist
  H arrest
  J delete

5 <u>migrate</u> with many others

  A move
  B remain
  C disagree
  D build

6 <u>blunt</u> answer

  F correct
  G difficult
  H long and detailed
  J short and rude

7 <u>ordinary</u> people

  A unusual
  B normal
  C kind
  D surprising

8 feel <u>relieved</u>

  F satisfied
  G without worry
  H angry about
  J concerned

Examples

Directions: Read the directions carefully. For items A and 1-2, choose the answer you think is correct. For items B and 3-5, choose the word that fits in both sentences.

A | **Part of this puzzle is missing.**

In which sentence does the word <u>part</u> mean the same thing as in the sentence above?

A On which side do you <u>part</u> your hair?

B Marcello has a small <u>part</u> in the play.

C This is an important <u>part</u> of the engine.

D Mix one <u>part</u> of juice to three of water.

B You can _____ the flowers there.

Is this the right _____ ?

F put
G place
H location
J arrange

Use the meaning of the sentences to find the right answer.

Check your answer one last time before you mark the circle.

Practice

1 | **This <u>column</u> of numbers is wrong.**

In which sentence does the word <u>column</u> mean the same thing as in the sentence above?

A The <u>column</u> of soldiers marched by.

B A large <u>column</u> held up the roof.

C Janna's newspaper <u>column</u> was funny.

D The research results were arranged in a single <u>column</u>.

2 | **This river begins as a small <u>spring</u>.**

In which sentence does the word <u>spring</u> mean the same thing as in the sentence above?

F We found a cool <u>spring</u> beside the trail.

G The lid was held shut by a <u>spring</u>.

H The rescue workers can <u>spring</u> into action quickly.

J A mountain goat will often <u>spring</u> from rock to rock.

3 My aunt was recently promoted to the rank of _____ in the U.S. Air Force.

I know the _____ area near camp.

A general
B major
C immediate
D approximate

4 The plane will _____ between five and six o'clock tonight.

How much _____ do you own?

F arrive
G property
H come
J land

5 You can earn _____ on your money.

Her greatest _____ is African art.

A profits
B enjoyment
C payment
D interest

STOP

Examples   **Directions:** Read the paragraph. Find the word below the paragraph that fits best in each numbered blank.

The ____(A)____ of our new house is beside a lake. Several other houses are nearby, but they are ____(B)____ by tall trees. The families who live near the lake have the right to use it for swimming and boating.

A   A   site
    B   mortgage
    C   approach
    D   door

B   F   populated
    G   aligned
    H   censored
    J   concealed

   **If you aren't sure which answer is correct, substitute each answer in the blank.**

Practice

The legal system that governs our actions today is ____(1)____ from several ____(2)____ . Much of our legal system comes from English common law. This body of law was ____(3)____ created by the kings that ruled after 1100 A.D. Another contribution from England was the *Magna Carta*, a ____(4)____ that stated that everyone, including the king himself, was subject to the law. The most ____(5)____ source of our legal system is the Constitution. It ____(6)____ everything from the branches of government to the age required to run for President.

1   A   attached
    B   situated
    C   derived
    D   serviced

4   F   document
    G   motion
    H   fiction
    J   sponsor

2   F   topics
    G   sources
    H   regions
    J   possibilities

5   A   realistic
    B   ferocious
    C   needless
    D   noteworthy

3   A   finally
    B   recently
    C   hopefully
    D   initially

6   F   blames
    G   specifies
    H   offends
    J   detects

Examples

Directions: Read each question. Fill in the circle for the answer you think is correct.

A Which of these words probably comes from the Latin word *manus* meaning *hand*?

A minimize
B measurable
C manage
D motion

B Businesses now _____ important papers before throwing them away.

Which of these words would indicate that the papers were cut into pieces?

F bolt
G shred
H slam
J fix

Stay with your first answer. It is right more often than it is wrong.

Practice

1 Which of these words probably comes from the French word *étage* meaning *a place to stand*?

A eaten
B attempt
C stranger
D stage

2 Which of these words probably comes from the Italian word *corriere* meaning *to run*?

F control
G court
H courier
J count

3 The family of the injured child found the newspaper reports _____ .

Which of these words means the family did not like the reports?

A offensive
B insatiable
C enlightened
D customary

4 The _____ was almost empty.

Which of these words would indicate that the food closet was almost empty?

F oven
G trunk
H pantry
J purse

For numbers 5 and 6, choose the answer that best defines the underlined part.

5 fish**ery**   print**ery**

A time when
B place where
C with
D almost

6 **aqua**rium   **aqua**tic

F pertaining to water
G pertaining to air
H without fear
J without speed

STOP

Examples

Directions: For items E1 and 1-8, find the word or words that mean the same or almost the same as the underlined word. For item E-2, mark the answer you think is correct.

E1 similar clothes

   A different
   B expensive
   C dull
   D alike

E2 Which of these probably comes from the Old French word *trenchier* meaning *to cut*?

   F trench
   G triangle
   H traffic
   J intricate

---

1 large structure

   A mountain
   B window
   C building
   D vehicle

2 unusual weather

   F abnormal
   G unpleasant
   H normal
   J good

3 delay her trip

   A enjoy
   B afford
   C hasten
   D postpone

4 be cautious

   F reckless
   G calm
   H careful
   J happy

5 A person who is eager —

   A is exhausted
   B came late for something
   C missed an opportunity
   D is enthusiastic

6 To dispense is to —

   F come out
   G give out
   H throw away
   J save money for

7 Prior means —

   A coming before
   B waiting beside
   C following closely
   D in place of

8 If something is humorous it is —

   F obvious
   G subtle
   H funny
   J boring

GO

9 Andy was <u>injured</u> in the baseball game.

To be <u>injured</u> is to be —

A good
B excited
C tired
D hurt

10 The South American hunter carried his <u>spear</u> proudly.

A <u>spear</u> is a —

F weapon
G hat
H prize
J shield

11 The deer seemed to <u>vanish</u> into the woods.

To <u>vanish</u> is to —

A jump
B disappear
C walk
D emerge

12 In the box was a <u>delicate</u> piece of glass.

If something is <u>delicate</u> it is —

F beautiful
G very expensive
H easily broken
J sturdy

13 She has a <u>temporary</u> job as a cook.

<u>Temporary</u> means —

A for a long time
B difficult
C relaxing
D for a short time

For numbers 14-19, find the word that means the opposite of the underlined word.

14 brief <u>pause</u>

F journey
G break
H inspection
J continuation

15 will <u>accumulate</u>

A evaluate
B suspend
C distribute
D stockpile

16 <u>corrupt</u> person

F comical
G honest
H competitive
J crooked

17 known <u>formerly</u>

A before
B widely
C personally
D currently

18 <u>slender</u> branch

F thick
G thin
H strong
J weak

19 <u>vital</u> mission

A unimportant
B essential
C strong
D irate

GO

For numbers 20-23, choose the word that correctly completes <u>both</u> sentences.

20 We need a new _____ in the kitchen.

The _____ of scores was 70 to 100.

F oven
G span
H range
J table

21 The woods are _____ here.

The ice was not very_____ .

A pretty
B thick
C hard
D dark

22 The _____ house is ours.

In a _____, the bird was gone.

F second
G last
H minute
J small

23 We should _____ this tire now.

A _____ of flowers was near the door.

A fix
B bunch
C patch
D replace

24 | If you park there, you will **block** the driveway.

In which sentence does the word <u>block</u> mean the same thing as in the sentence above?

F You can <u>block</u> the door with this brick.

G Our <u>block</u> has some great trees.

H Jean's brother carved this <u>block</u> of wood into the shape of a cat.

J We bought a <u>block</u> of tickets to the game.

25 | <u>State</u> your name and address.

In which sentence does the word <u>state</u> mean the same thing as in the sentence above?

A Each <u>state</u> has its own capital.

B Her <u>state</u> of mind was positive when she started the race.

C When you <u>state</u> your position, speak clearly.

D The old farmhouse was in a poor <u>state</u>.

For numbers 26 and 27, choose the answer that best defines the underlined part.

26 <u>dis</u>place   <u>dis</u>charge

F not
G almost
H away from
J in the direction of

27 civi<u>lize</u>   crystal<u>lize</u>

A to become
B to weaken
C very much
D instead of

GO

28 Which of these words probably comes from the Latin word *tolerare* meaning *to bear pain*?

F tool
G total
H tolerate
J torture

29 Which of these words probably comes from the Old English word *bindan* meaning *to tie*?

A bind
B band
C bend
D blind

30 The _____ for animals is often improved by sensible development.

Which of these words means the place where animals live?

F garment
G habitat
H tropical
J treasury

31 An _____ bystander identified the criminal.

Which of these words means the person paid attention to what he or she saw?

A splendid
B fidgety
C instinctive
D observant

Read the paragraph. Find the word below the paragraph that fits best in each numbered blank.

Manufacturing has changed ___(32)___ in the last hundred years. Around the turn of the ___(33)___ , manufacturing required much hand labor. When machines were used, they were powered by steam or water. Today, much less human labor is required because ___(34)___ machines do so much of the work. Most contemporary manufacturing equipment is powered by electricity, and you rarely see the ___(35)___ of steam that signaled a nineteenth-century factory.

32 F little
    G confusingly
    H hastily
    J considerably

33 A decade
    B time
    C century
    D age

34 F precision
    G ominous
    H overgrown
    J recognition

35 A plateaus
    B plumes
    C trifles
    D wads

STOP

Examples   Directions: For item E1, find the word that means the same or almost the same as the underlined word. For item E2, mark the answer you think is correct. Then, follow the directions for each part of this test.

E1 <u>daring</u> rescue A foolish B rapid C brave D painstaking	**E2** **Which of these probably comes from the Old English word *fikol* meaning *deceitful*?** F frank G infinity H definitely J fickle

For numbers 1–13, find the word or words that mean the same or almost the same as the underlined word.

1   slight <u>gesture</u>

   A distance
   B movement
   C build
   D angle

2   tightly <u>bound</u>

   F boxed
   G released
   H matched
   J tied

3   <u>deny</u> him permission

   A allow
   B give
   C offer
   D refuse

4   <u>link</u> the ideas

   F separate
   G join
   H identify
   J like

5   To <u>support</u> is to —

   A not enjoy
   B not play
   C let down
   D hold up

6   <u>Cardiac</u> refers to the —

   F brain
   G stomach
   H heart
   J foot

7   A <u>cottage</u> is a —

   A castle
   B garage
   C huge barn
   D small house

8   To <u>irritate</u> is to —

   F contact
   G bother
   H chase
   J embarrass

GO

9   Georgina <u>stumbled</u> on the path.

Stumbled means —

A   jumped
B   walked
C   ran
D   tripped

10   Your <u>response</u> was too short.

Response means the same as —

F   answer
G   story
H   paragraph
J   problem

11   The hotel had a wonderful <u>staff</u>.

A staff is a —

A   swimming pool
B   group of workers
C   lobby
D   restaurant

12   Donna told us a <u>brief</u> story.

Brief means —

F   sad
G   funny
H   long
J   short

13   Ken <u>stored</u> the children's toys.

Stored means —

A   found
B   wrapped
C   put away
D   bought

For numbers 14-19, find the word that means the opposite of the underlined word.

14   the <u>proper</u> tools

F   incorrect
G   useful
H   appropriate
J   adjustable

15   might <u>detain</u>

A   hold
B   release
C   enlighten
D   restrain

16   seems <u>colorful</u>

F   pale
G   vibrant
H   delightful
J   humid

17   <u>reveal</u> the truth

A   make known
B   look for
C   disbelieve
D   carefully hide

18   <u>persist</u> for a while

F   continue
G   resist
H   cease
J   follow

19   <u>sufficient</u> for now

A   too expensive
B   too little
C   enough
D   unnecessary

GO

For numbers 20-23, choose the word that correctly completes <u>both</u> sentences.

20 The _____ was a few minutes late.

Gina will _____ hard for the race.

  F bus
  G practice
  H train
  J plane

21 How much _____ do you have?

Remember to _____ your wet shoes.

  A money
  B change
  C adjust
  D wind

22 The worker carried a _____ .

Let's _____ some apples.

  F pick
  G bake
  H shovel
  J ladder

23 Cheryl put the _____ on the shelf.

The swimming _____ was just broken.

  A video
  B pool
  C package
  D record

24 | **What grade did you get in math?**

In which sentence does the word <u>grade</u> mean the same thing as in the sentence above?

  F This store offers only the top grade of fruits and vegetables.

  G The best way to improve my grade is to study harder.

  H The grade on this hill is so steep that trucks find it difficult.

  J Mrs. Irwin will grade our papers today.

25 | **Randi made her <u>point</u> by giving several examples.**

In which sentence does the word <u>point</u> mean the same thing as in the sentence above?

  A Grant broke the point on his pencil.

  B The point of his argument is that the park is good for the town.

  C The point of the compass changed as the boat made a turn.

  D Can you point to the right store?

For numbers 26 and 27, choose the answer that best defines the underlined part.

26 <u>pre</u>judge   <u>pre</u>school

  F after
  G less than
  H more than
  J before

27 cloud<u>y</u>   itch<u>y</u>

  A inclined to be
  B not
  C much
  D about to become

GO

28 Which of these words probably comes from the Latin word *fimbri* meaning *a border*?

   F family
   G fringe
   H image
   J feminine

29 Which of these words probably comes from the Old French word *renc* meaning *row*?

   A wrench
   B rich
   C rank
   D prank

30 We made sure the house was _____ before we left for vacation.

   Which of these words means the house was locked up tightly?

   F sincere
   G vacated
   H secure
   J inevitable

31 It began to _____ so we packed everything up and went home.

   Which of these words means it began to rain just a little?

   A drizzle
   B downpour
   C dazzle
   D thwart

Read the paragraph. Find the word below the paragraph that fits best in each numbered blank.

Inventions don't have to be ___(32)___ to be successful. A good example of a simple invention is the water-filled barrels that serve as protective ___(33)___ at a highway bridge or overpass. Another is the Frisbee®, a toy that sells millions of ___(34)___ a year. And of course, there's the ultimate in simplicity, the clothespin. These examples demonstrate that clever individuals don't need huge corporations or a research ___(35)___ to come up with good ideas.

32 **F** elaborate
   G cancelled
   H comprehensible
   J sincere

33 **A** frontiers
   B barriers
   C parcels
   D testimonials

34 **F** arbors
   G notions
   H licenses
   J units

35 **A** attitude
   B perspective
   C facility
   D harness

STOP

Example   **Directions:** Read each item. Choose the answer you think is
correct. Mark the space for your answer.

Near the beach, secluded among the sand dunes, was a small freshwater pond. It was fed by a spring and remained cool even during the hottest summer days. The plants and animals that made their homes around the spring were unusual for this part of the state.	**A** **What part of a story does this passage tell about?** **A** the plot **B** the characters **C** the mood **D** the setting

 **If a question sounds confusing, try to restate it to yourself in
simpler terms. Be sure you understand the question before you
choose an answer.**

Practice

1 **Which of these probably came from a
geography book?**

  A During Jefferson's presidency, America
  greatly expanded its borders.

  B Dirt is primarily composed of clay, silt,
  and sand.

  C Natural features often form the border
  between countries.

  D The principles that keep a plane aloft
  are easy to understand.

2 **Kim is reading a story about a woman
pioneer in the American West after the
Civil War. Which of these is most likely
to be the beginning of the story?**

  F Susan kissed her parents good-bye and
  boarded the train.

  G When she arrived in Deadwood, Susan
  was amazed at what she saw.

  H This was Susan's tenth year in the
  mountains.

  J The friends she had made among the
  ranchers supported Susan's ideas.

3   Washington, DC, has everything for the
visitor, from famous monuments and
museums to boating on the Potomac.

  **A passage like this would most likely be
  found in a —**

  A fable.

  B biography.

  C history book.

  D traveler's guide.

4 **Which of these descriptions of a festival
states an opinion?**

  F This is the twentieth year the festival
  has been held.

  G This year's festival is the best ever.

  H More people attended the festival this
  year than ever before.

  J The festival was held in the town park.

Example

Directions: Read the passage. Find the best answer to each question that follows the passage.

Gardeners around the country are discovering the virtues of grass. Not the kind you mow, but large, decorative grasses that are close cousins of the sprouts in the typical lawn. Ornamental grasses have a number of advantages: they require little water, deer don't eat them, they grow quickly, and they come in a number of beautiful varieties.

A **Which of these is an advantage of ornamental grasses?**

  A Quick growth

  B Eaten by deer

  C Beautiful flowers

  D Grow in moist soil

Look for key words in the question, then find the same words in the passage. This will help you locate the correct answer.

Practice

Here is a story about a girl's feeling when she first encountered a mountain lion. Read the story and then do numbers 1 through 8 on page 122.

When we moved to a small town a few hours from Denver, I didn't think much about it. We had lived in small towns before, and I kind of liked them. It wasn't as exciting as living in the city or the suburbs, but it wasn't bad. The kids were great, and I enjoyed doing lots of things outdoors.

A few weeks after we moved into our house, I heard a terrible sound around sundown that froze my blood. It sounded like an animal screaming. My mother said it was probably a mountain lion, and my heart almost stopped. A mountain lion was close enough to our house for me to hear it. I was terrified.

The next day in school, I asked some of my friends about it. They said there were a few mountain lions in the area, but they didn't bother anyone. Occasionally, a lion would kill a calf or sheep on a farm, but they pretty much stayed away from the town and the houses around it. None of them had ever seen a mountain lion, but all of them had heard one.

I heard the lion again often, but never saw it...that is, until I was hiking with my family a few months later. We had gotten an early start and were heading up a trail beside a canyon. My father told us to stop and be quiet. He pointed across the canyon and there it was. The lion was lying on a ledge, enjoying the warmth of the first rays of the sun. It looked almost like a house cat finding a sunny spot on the floor.

We watched the great cat for a few minutes and then began walking up the trail. As soon as we started moving, the lion jumped up and stared at us. For a few seconds he looked right at me, and I was surprised that I felt no fear. It was almost as if the cat understood that I posed no threat, that I was just another creature in the mountains. Then, with a few great leaps, the cat disappeared over a ridge.

I never saw the big cat again. It's a funny thing, though. I began thinking of the mountain lion as mine, and whenever I heard it calling in the night, I was sure it was letting me know it was all right.

GO

1   **According to the story, which of these is true about the narrator?**

A   She prefers small towns to cities.

B   She dislikes cities.

C   She dislikes small towns.

D   She prefers cities to small towns.

2   **How did the narrator feel about the mountain lion at the end of the story?**

F   Frightened

G   Indifferent

H   Possessive

J   Abandoned

3   **Which of these would be most likely to dislike a mountain lion?**

A   A hiker

B   A store owner

C   A farmer

D   A student

4   **In the story, the phrase "froze my blood" means —**

F   the narrator was frightened.

G   the narrator was cold.

H   the father was angry.

J   the mother was alarmed.

5   **The narrator in this story —**

A   saw the mountain lion before hearing it.

B   heard the mountain lion before seeing it.

C   followed the mountain lion.

D   became concerned about farm animals.

6   **The mountain lion is compared to a —**

F   hunting wolf.

G   dog curled up on a pillow.

H   snake ready to strike.

J   cat in a sunny spot.

7   **Which of these statements about mountain lions is true, according to the story?**

A   Mountain lions are only found in the mountains.

B   Mountain lions generally avoid people.

C   Mountain lions occasionally "adopt" human families.

D   Mountain lions prefer cold weather.

8   **The narrator learned about mountain lions from —**

F   her mother.

G   her father.

H   friends at school.

J   a library book.

GO

As part of a pen pal project, Ashihiro kept a journal of what the weather was like on the first day of every month for his friend in Argentina. Use the journal to do numbers 9-16. on page 124.

January 1   The ground is covered with about an inch of snow. It is very cold, about 10°, but the sun is shining and the sky is perfectly blue. The wind is blowing at about ten miles an hour from the west. Clouds are supposed to start moving in this afternoon.

February 1   I can't believe how warm it is, almost 40°. There are a few clouds, but it is mostly sunny. The high today is going to be almost 60°. This warm weather is something we call the "January thaw," but this year it happened in February instead.

March 1   This is probably the most miserable day of the year. It's raining, cloudy, and the wind is blowing. I'm glad it's Saturday. Whenever we have weather like this on the weekend my computer gets a good workout.

April 1   It snowed almost 10 inches last night! Only kidding…it's an April Fool's Day joke. Today is beautiful, and my friends and I are going to the park to play baseball. I play the outfield and am pretty good, but not as good as my older sister.

May 1   The wind is really blowing and a storm is coming in. The weather report says we might have thunder and lightning for the first time this year. I love storms, as long as I can be inside.

June 1   School will be over in two more weeks! I hope the weather all summer is like this. The temperature is supposed to be 70° and there isn't a cloud in the sky. I'll be staring out the window in school all day.

July 1   What a dreadful day! The temperature is already 80°, it's damp and sticky, and there isn't a breeze anywhere. I wish we had a swimming pool, but living in the city in an apartment makes that impossible.

August 1   The weather has finally started to cool off. All of July was humid, almost exactly like the day I wrote you. It was impossible to sleep at night because it was so sticky. I hope it stays cool for a while.

September 1   School starts in four days…yuck. If the weather then is as miserable as it is today, I might not even go. Actually, I love the first day of school because I get to see everyone and it's so busy we don't have much work.

October 1   The fall colors have been spectacular, and today is a perfect day to enjoy them. The sky is blue, there are just a few clouds, and the sun is bright. I feel sorry for people who don't have trees that change color in the fall.

November 1   Winter is definitely here. It's cold, gray, and in general, nasty. The temperature is still in the 20°s, and I'm not looking forward to school at all. I have to walk to school, and I hate getting there wet.

December 1   When December rolls around, everyone in school starts thinking about the holidays. This year, everyone is thinking about the weather. We have had the snowiest winter in history. It's like living in Alaska. Two feet of snow fell last night, and there was already a foot on the ground. Pretty soon, we'll have to dig tunnels to get around.

GO

9 What can you conclude about where the writer of this journal lives?

A It is usually warm.

B It is usually cold.

C It has good weather.

D It has four seasons.

10 What is the "January thaw"?

F A surprising cold spell that usually takes place in January

G An unusually cold January

H A surprising warm spell that usually takes place in January

J An unusually warm winter

11 How do the journal entries change from January to December?

A They focus less on the weather than on the writer's feelings.

B They become much shorter.

C They talk more about the writer's family.

D They focus more on the weather than on the writer's feelings.

12 To Ashihiro, the weather in July is —

F cooler than usual.

G too hot and sticky.

H just right for outdoor activities.

J better than in the fall.

13 How does the writer feel about the first day of school?

A Bored about school

B Excited to go

C Sad that summer is over

D Happy to go to a new school

14 What does the writer mean in the March first entry when he says his "computer will get a good workout"?

F He will work hard to earn money to buy a computer.

G He will go to the gym before using his computer.

H He will spend the day using the computer.

J He will work out instead of using his computer.

15 How does Ashihiro get to school?

A By walking

B By school bus

C By public bus

D By car

16 In the entry for September first, what does the word "miserable" mean?

F Pleasant

G Unusual

H Usual

J Unpleasant

Example

Directions: Read the passage. Find the best answer to each question that follows the passage.

An unusual presidential election took place in 1789; it was the first election in the history of the United States. General George Washington ran without opposition and was chosen *unanimously* by the electors from every state. Ironically, Washington almost refused to run for office!	**A What is the meaning of the word "unanimously" in this passage?** **A** By most electors **B** By a few electors **C** By all electors **D** By exactly half the electors

Skim the passage so you have an understanding of what it is about. Then skim the questions. Answer the easiest questions first, and look back at the passage to find the answer.

Practice

Here is a passage about a misunderstanding among family members. Read the passage and then do numbers 1 through 7 on page 126.

A Family's Fright

The Dunn family and friends had gathered for a barbecue. Amy and her friend Nicole were the only young people, and they soon tired of the adult conversation, so they went off to amuse themselves. They practiced twirling a metal rod that regularly fell with a loud clang, causing the people on the porch to jump at each crash.

"You kids, go play on the sand where that thing will not make so much noise," Amy's mother said impatiently.

"On the sand across the street, or on the sand down the way?" Amy asked.

"Wherever," was the absentminded answer, and she turned back to the conversation.

As darkness fell on the pleasant evening, the guests began to leave. Someone asked about the girls. "Oh, they must be in the house," Amy's mother answered with a shrug.

"I don't see them," someone else called back.

That was enough to have Mrs. Dunn on her feet in an instant. "Aim-eee, Ni-cole," she called upstairs and down, in the front yard and back. She grabbed a flashlight and raced out of the house and down the street, thoroughly frightened now.

The others waited and watched for the beam of light to pierce the darkness, signaling that the three were on their way back. It seemed like hours, but was only minutes when they appeared at the end of the street.

Amy's mother put an arm around each girl. "Don't ever do that to me again, please."

"But, Mom, you said we could go down there," Amy protested.

"You knew better than to stay so long..." The sentence remained unfinished, but all three knew what she meant. The girls' protests and explanations also dissolved in the hug. All three were laughing as they approached the house. The adults on the porch were mystified, but their relief was great enough to keep them quiet.

GO

1 **What would be another good title for this story?**

A "A Close Call"

B "Kids Will Be Kids"

C "A Family Gathering"

D "A Bad Decision"

2 **Why did Amy's mother tell the girls to go play in another place?**

F They were being noisy.

G She did not want them out too late.

H The other adults asked her to.

J There were no other young people there.

3 **Why did the girls stop trying to explain why they had gone so far away?**

A They did not care what Mrs. Dunn thought.

B They did not have a good reason for staying out so late.

C They knew they were going to be punished anyway.

D They realized how worried Mrs. Dunn had been and how relieved she was now.

4 **Which of these sentences would best fit at the end of the story?**

F The other adults didn't think Mrs. Dunn handled the situation very well.

G Nicole called her mother and asked to go home right away.

H Amy and Nicole decided to be more careful the next time they went to play.

J Mrs. Dunn was too embarrassed to visit with the other people.

5 **The girls wandered off because they —**

A wanted to see the beach.

B were looking for a kitten.

C were waiting to eat.

D were bored.

6 **When Mrs. Dunn said "Wherever," it showed that she —**

F wasn't really paying attention.

G wanted the children to go away.

H was worried about the children.

J hadn't heard what the girls said.

7 **This story began —**

A in the morning.

B around sunset.

C around noon.

D late in the night.

GO

Spectrum Vocabulary Grade 6

A Stupid Thing to Do

"Is that you, Enrique?" called Mr. Torres from his big chair in front of the television.

"Yeah, it's me, Dad," answered Enrique as he shut the front door behind him.

"Come in here a minute, Son, I want to talk to you," said Mr. Torres.

Enrique sighed and slowly walked toward his father with his hands in his pockets. "I really need to do something in my room, Dad."

"Listen, Enrique. Isn't it a little late for you to be coming home from Lloyd Carlson's house? I know it's a Friday night, and there is no school tomorrow, but I don't like you out on the streets at this hour."

"Hey, Dad, the Carlsons just live in the next block. It's not like I've been walking all over town," replied Enrique, gesturing with his hands.

"What's that on your hands, Son?" asked Mr. Torres.

Enrique looked at his hands and saw streaks of blue paint. "Oh, Lloyd and I were working on some models. I guess I wasn't very careful with the paint."

"Okay, Enrique, off to bed. We'll talk about this more tomorrow. I don't want you out on the streets when it gets this late, even if it's just a block away. Things happen."

Mr. Torres turned off the television and sat in his chair thinking about his son. He sighed, then he went out to the garage to see if the door was closed before he went to bed. He noticed that the can of blue spray paint was not on the shelf where it belonged.

The next morning, Mr. Torres called the Carlsons on the telephone. When he finished speaking to Mrs. Carlson, he hung up the phone and sat drinking a cup of coffee until Enrique came into the kitchen for breakfast.

"Well, good morning, Son," said Mr. Torres with a smile. "You and Lloyd are in for a big surprise next Saturday. There's a very special event taking place in town, and the Carlsons and I have signed you two boys up."

Enrique's face lit up. "What is it, Dad? A Bike-a-thon? A basketball game? Is a celebrity coming to town?"

"No, Son," said Mr. Torres. "None of those things. It's our city's third annual Paint the Town Day. About a thousand people are getting together to paint over graffiti that has been spray painted on walls, fences, and buildings. The only celebrity you're likely to see is the mayor, who is handing out 5,000 gallons of paint and brushes for this project."

Enrique's face fell. "You know, huh?"

"Yes, Enrique. Lloyd's parents thought you boys were over here last night. When I told them I thought you were over there, we figured out what you had done. My first impulse was to call the police, but Mr. Carlson suggested we give you one more chance. On the phone this morning we came up with this idea as a suitable way for you boys to pay the community back for what you have done," said his father. "Graffiti makes our city look bad and costs a lot of money to clean up. So next Saturday, you and Lloyd are going to put in a long day's work."

"Okay, Dad. It was a stupid thing to do, and I'm really sorry. Lloyd and I never did anything like that before, and I promise we won't ever do it again. Next Saturday, we'll be the two best painters in town. You can count on it."

GO >

8 Why did Mr. Torres want to talk to Enrique when he came in the door on Friday night?

   F He had a surprise for Enrique.

   G He wanted some company.

   H Enrique was late coming home.

   J Enrique had blue paint on his hands.

9 How did Mr. Torres feel when he saw the can of blue spray paint was gone?

   A Suspicious

   B Relieved

   C Angry

   D Sad

10 "Paint the Town" is an example of —

   F a way to punish young people who have done bad things.

   G a way to celebrate the founding of the town.

   H an opportunity for people to paint their houses with the town's paint.

   J a community project to make the town a better place to live.

11 In this story, what is a "fitting punishment"?

   A One that is easy for the boys to do

   B One that fits the boys' plans

   C One that suits the crime

   D One that is difficult for the boys to do

12 What do Mr. Torres and the Carlsons hope to do with their plan?

   F Teach Enrique and Lloyd to be responsible for what they have done

   G Make the boys angry because they have been caught

   H Help the boys understand the importance of coming home on time

   J Make the boys stay home at night and do their homework

13 Why does Mr. Torres worry about Enrique?

   A His school grades are getting lower.

   B He often gets in trouble with Lloyd.

   C Bad things can happen late at night.

   D The boys need their sleep.

14 When Mr. Torres says he has a surprise for the boys, Enrique —

   F thinks it is something fun to do.

   G worries that he has been caught.

   H wants to call Lloyd to let him know.

   J becomes angry because he has been punished.

15 How does Enrique feel when he learns he is going to "Paint the Town"?

   A Relieved because he hasn't been caught

   B Sorry for doing the wrong thing

   C Angry because he is being punished

   D Annoyed that his father suspected him

GO ▷

The Ocean

Nearly three-fourths of the earth is covered by the oceans. Traditionally, there are said to be five oceans: Atlantic, Pacific, Indian, Arctic, and Antarctic. In reality, all are interconnected, and people, fish, and sea mammals move easily among them. The boundaries of the oceans are loosely determined by islands and land masses, and the terms sea, gulf, and bay are used for subdivisions of the oceans.

Ocean water is salty because of dissolved minerals, and it is the nourishing environment for a host of living things. Plants use the dissolved chemicals that are washed into the oceans for their growth. Tiny animals eat the plants, and larger animals eat them. People eventually eat these large fish, so, in a sense, the minerals in ocean water also nourish us.

Oceans are not alone in being salty. Several "seas"—the Dead Sea, the Caspian Sea, and the Great Salt Lake—are also salty. Dissolved minerals flow into these inland seas, which do not have outlets with other bodies of water. When the sun evaporates the water in these lakes, the concentration of minerals rises, making the lakes salty.

The saltiness in oceans and lakes varies greatly from place to place. Places where the water is confined by islands or peninsulas are saltier than the open water. In the open water, the wind and currents keep the minerals from becoming too concentrated in one place.

Ocean water moves constantly because of currents, wind, and tides. Currents are great rivers within the oceans. One of the best known is the Gulf Stream, which is warm and moves along the southern coast of the United States. Tides are movements of water determined by the positions of the sun, moon, and earth. The gravitational pull of the sun and moon make the water move toward and away from the land in a regular pattern. Wind moves water irregularly, as anyone can tell from watching the waves swell up, turn into a curve, and splash down in a foamy spray.

Humans are closely attached to the ocean. Oceanographers study it and plan ways for people to use it better. Ecologists worry that we will pollute the oceans and damage the fragile life there. Vacationers are soothed by the sights and sounds of the ocean and beach. Sportsmen test themselves against its fish. The ocean is interesting, entertaining, mysterious, and absolutely necessary for life on earth.

GO >

16 **What causes movement of water in the oceans?**

   F Concentrated minerals left by evaporation

   G Natural weather events

   H Fish and people sailing in boats

   J Rivers at the bottom of all the oceans

17 **Why is the water in the Dead Sea, the Caspian Sea, and the Great Salt Lake saltier than the ocean?**

   A They are warmer than the oceans.

   B The land around them is saltier.

   C They are smaller than the other oceans.

   D There is no outlet for their waters.

18 **According to this article, the oceans are necessary for —**

   F life.

   G travel.

   H fun.

   J communication.

19 **If you wanted to learn more about the ocean, you should —**

   A read a fishing or boating magazine.

   B look up the definition of "currents" in the dictionary.

   C check the library card catalog under the topic "ocean."

   D find the encyclopedia entry titled "water."

20 **Based on what you have read in the passage, an appropriate name for the earth would be —**

   F The Desert Planet.

   G The Cloud Planet.

   H The Evaporation Planet.

   J The Water Planet.

21 **Which statement is an *opinion* in the article?**

   A There are five oceans: Atlantic, Pacific, Indian, Arctic, and Antarctic.

   B The ocean is interesting, entertaining, mysterious, and necessary.

   C Saltiness increases as evaporation occurs.

   D The water of landlocked seas is saltier than ocean water.

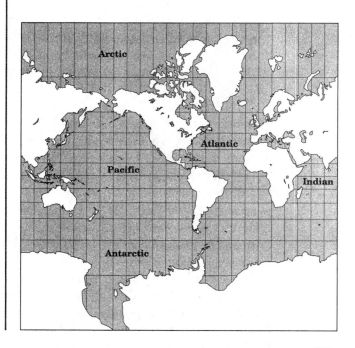

Example   Directions: Read the selection then mark the answer you think is correct.

A group of people stood around a puddle on the ground. From the puddle spilled a small stream of water. They were all amazed, for the puddle and stream had come from nowhere. During the night, a spring had appeared in the park, and no one knew what had caused it.

A   The people were probably —

  A frightened.
  B curious.
  C angry.
  D elated.

Here is a passage about two actors who could terrorize an audience. Read the story and then do numbers 1 through 6 on page 132.

Horror movies today are filled with special effects created by computers and mechanical devices. In the early years of film, however, there were no such artificial methods. The actors themselves had to frighten the audience, and the two who were the best at it were Lon Chaney and Bela Lugosi.

The son of deaf parents, Lon Chaney learned Sign Language early in his life and became adept at making himself known through gestures and pantomime. He had little formal education, but at that time—he was born in 1883—an education wasn't as important as it is today. He worked at odd jobs around his home in Colorado Springs, Colorado, and became interested in the theater while working as a stage hand. Chaney tried his hand at playwriting and vaudeville, eventually working his way to Hollywood.

In the *Miracle Man*, which was released in 1919, Lon Chaney made his first appearance as a monster. His reputation grew enormously when he played Quasimodo in the 1923 version of *The Hunchback of Notre Dame*, and he went on to star in other successful films. Chaney only had one speaking role, since films during this era were silent, and was able to capture his audience through the expert application of makeup, the use of gestures, and an uncanny knack for adopting the personality of the monsters he played.

Bela Lugosi's story is quite different. Born in eastern Europe in 1884, Lugosi studied at the Academy of Theatrical Art in Budapest. He worked as an actor in the theatre for years, and when World War I broke out, served as an officer in the Hungarian army. He fled his country in the turmoil that followed the war and emigrated to the United States.

Lugosi resumed his career as an actor in both plays and films after he arrived in New York. He was moderately successful, but he achieved stardom playing the vampire in the 1931 movie *Dracula*. He starred in a string of horror films that remain cult classics even to this day among late-night television viewers and old movie fans.

Like Chaney, Lugosi "became" his characters. With his eastern European accent and mysterious looks, he was the perfect Dracula. In his other films, his evil characters were always more believable than anyone else's, and crowds were drawn to his movies to see this star who appeared to be the heart of evil.

GO ▷

1   **Which of these did Lon Chaney and Bela Lugosi have in common?**

   A   They both studied at a famous school of theater.

   B   Their parents helped them to become actors.

   C   They both had unusual accents.

   D   They were born within a year of each other.

2   **According to the passage, Lon Chaney —**

   F   got his start acting in New York City.

   G   made most of his films during the silent era.

   H   starred with Bela Lugosi in just one movie.

   J   first appeared in the film *The Hunchback of Notre Dame*.

3   **Which of these probably helped Bela Lugosi get the part of Dracula?**

   A   Lugosi had experience in the war.

   B   Both the character Dracula and Lugosi were the same height.

   C   The Dracula character was from eastern Europe, so Lugosi sounded like him.

   D   Lugosi was popular among television viewers.

4   **The writer of this passage believes that —**

   F   horror movies today depend more on special effects than acting ability.

   G   silent movies are better than movies where the actors can speak.

   H   theatrical training is an important ingredient in stage success.

   J   horror movies are the best kind of film.

5   **This passage says that Lon Chaney had "an uncanny knack for adopting the personality of the monsters he played." The word *uncanny* means —**

   A   beyond the ordinary.

   B   eastern European.

   C   natural.

   D   limited.

6   **The author suggests that Bela Lugosi was so successful because —**

   F   his accent sounded evil.

   G   fans were less sophisticated years ago.

   H   he appeared to be the heart of evil.

   J   films are too technical today.

GO >

Butch's Discount City
1410 Main Street

Annual Summer Clearance
As the temperatures rise, the prices fall!

Deluxe Ceiling Fan
with light kit
• 3-speed
• quiet
• reversible
only $35.97

Garden Rain Sprinkler
Model 3600
"Makes your lawn
beautiful"
was $8.96
reduced to $4.97

Boys' Short-Sleeved
T-Shirts
• solid colors
• s-m-l-xl
Regularly $3.00
Reduced to $1.50

Select group of ladies'
summer shoes and sandals
(on racks)
Name brands
40% off regular prices

Bertha's Bargain Bonanza
5331 Seventh Avenue

Always the best buys in town! (Sale prices good through Saturday)

All boys' shorts and shirts
on sale now, sizes 4-18
Giant blowout
25% off regular prices

Fourth of July
paper goods
Everything must go
half price

All electric fans in stock
now reduced 10%
(regularly $9.99-$49.99)

Flower seeds
Plant a late summer garden
(this year's seeds) 79¢ each

Store Hours: 9 A.M. - 7 P.M., Monday through Saturday

GO

7 **What time of year is it when these ads might appear in the newspaper?**

   A early spring

   B middle to late summer

   C winter

   D just before Thanksgiving

8 **What does "reversible" mean in the deluxe ceiling fan ad at Butch's?**

   F The light and the fan can run independently of each other.

   G The fan can be turned off and on.

   H The blades of the fan can be made to turn in opposite directions.

   J The fan will create heat in the winter.

9 **Both stores' advertisements stress —**

   A good service.

   B excellent location.

   C lengthy store hours.

   D bargain prices.

10 **You would most likely find these advertisements in a —**

   F gardening book.

   G national magazine.

   H telephone book.

   J local newspaper.

11 **In the ad for Butch's Discount City, the line "As the temperatures rise, the prices fall!" means that—**

   A Butch's usually has a sale in the summer.

   B prices are reduced any time the temperature reaches 100 degrees.

   C Butch's has lower prices than Bertha's.

   D Butch's does not have sales in cool weather.

12 **Which of these is an *opinion* in Bertha's ad?**

   F Plant a late summer garden

   G Sale prices good through Saturday

   H Always the best buys in town

   J Half price

13 **Which of these does *not* have an exact price specified?**

   A Deluxe ceiling fan

   B Ladies summer shoes and sandals

   C Boys short-sleeved t-shirts

   D Garden Rain Sprinkler

14 **The sale at Butch's Discount City is —**

   F a yearly event.

   G a weekly event.

   H a monthly event.

   J a daily event.

GO ⟩

Can fish smell fishermen?

Some people go fishing to enjoy the peace, quiet, and beauty of nature. Some love to catch fish for a tasty meal. Others, however, fish for sport and will go to great lengths to catch the most or the largest fish. Huge amounts of money and fabulous prizes are offered at some fishing contests. The bait, the equipment, the location all are important factors, but there is one additional thing to consider: fish have a remarkable sense of smell.

Bass have a well-developed *olfactory* sense. The older they get, the more they use their sense of smell. Catfish, trout, and other fish can also smell very well. Some things smell good to fish, and some things smell bad. Fishermen, then, must learn to avoid smells that turn away fish if they are going to win a competition.

Chewing tobacco and smoking, in addition to being bad for you, create an odor that fish don't like. Gasoline spilled in or on a boat will also repel fish. One of the worst turn-offs for fish is the chemical L-serine, which is present in human perspiration. This means fisherman should bathe before they go fishing and wear clean clothes.

Scientists have found that all people produce L-serine, but some create more than others. A group of the top professional tournament fishermen have been tested, and they seem to have very little L-serine in their perspiration.

There is no evidence that fish like the same perfumes that humans find attractive, however. Most tournament fishermen use plain soap, without perfume, to wash. They even take soap with them on their boats. Sporting goods stores also sell a spray that masks human odors and adds a smell that is supposed to appeal to fish.

Not everyone is a tournament fisherman, but most people like to catch fish when they go out on the lake. If you expect to catch fish, you can wear your old clothes and favorite hat, but be sure you are clean. Avoid tobacco—which everyone should do anyway—and wash off spilled gasoline. Don't chase away fish with bad smells.

GO

15 Which words from the article tell that some people don't care whether they catch fish or not?

   A ...enjoy the peace, quiet, and beauty...

   B ...huge amounts of money...

   C ...catch fish for a tasty meal.

   D ...most people like to catch fish...

16 As bass get older, they —

   F learn to like the smells of human beings.

   G become more like trout and catfish.

   H have less L-serine in their system.

   J depend more on their sense of smell.

17 What would be the best thing to do to answer Number 16?

   A Look closely at the first paragraph and then the last paragraph.

   B Read the title and think about what it means.

   C Skim the passage and look for the key words "bass" and "older."

   D Look up L-serine in the dictionary or encyclopedia.

18 What natural human odor do fish not like?

   F Gasoline

   G L-serine

   H Chemical attractants

   J Perfume

19 This passage is an example of which type of writing?

   A Providing information

   B Expressing an opinion

   C Fiction

   D A review

20 The author probably included the first sentence of the third paragraph because —

   F winning a fishing tournament is difficult if you smoke.

   G L-serine and tobacco have many of the same ingredients.

   H gasoline spilled in a boat will chase fish away.

   J in addition to scaring off fish, tobacco can harm your health.

21 In this passage, the word *olfactory* has something to do with —

   A fishing.

   B bass.

   C age.

   D smelling.

22 This passage is mostly about —

   F fishing tournaments.

   G an important fishing tip.

   H why people enjoy fishing.

   J differences between people and fish.

GO >

That Trophy Season

From their team name, the Aardvarks, to their uniforms, shorts and bowling shirts, the Lincoln School baseball team was unusual. They had gone years without winning a game, and because their school was so small, it had both girls and boys playing on the same team. Most of all, however, was the team attitude: they loved baseball. Every team they played admitted that, no matter how bad they were, the Aardvarks played their hearts out and were good sports.

A few years ago, however, something changed. A set of twins, Dot and Dash Morse, had started school in the fall, and to say they were great ball players was an understatement. They were fabulous. Dash could pitch like a high school player, and Dot played shortstop like she had been born there. Moreover, they had a great sense of humor, obviously inherited from their parents, who had named their children after the Morse code signals. They poked fun at everyone and everything, but nothing pleased them more than making fun of themselves.

All of this came as a surprise to Coach McNally, who had heard nothing about the Morse twins until the first day of spring training. He knew they were good students, as was everyone else on the Aardvarks baseball team, and welcomed them to tryouts. Within a few minutes, however, they had him scratching his head. He couldn't believe his good fortune: these two kids were the best he had ever seen. What was even better was that they had a great attitude toward the game and seemed to be infecting the other players. For the first time in years, Coach McNally actually began to think about winning games.

Throughout spring training, Coach McNally downplayed his squad's ability. All the players knew this was going to be a special year, but when asked about his team, the coach just said they were going to enjoy the game as much as ever. In his heart, however, he couldn't wait for the season to start.

On opening day, the Aardvarks faced the Mountaineers, a traditional powerhouse. Everyone in the stands anticipated the annual blowout, but when Dash threw his first pitch, the sound of his strike whacking the catcher's mitt got everyone's attention. And when the first three Mountaineers went down in order, even the opposing players suspected this was not going to be business as usual.

Dot was up first for the Aardvarks, and just like in the movies, sent a ball into the stands. The Aardvark fans went absolutely wild. It was the first time in anyone's memory they had a real reason to cheer. By the time the game was over, everyone at the game knew that the Aardvarks were the team to beat. Not only had Dot and Dash dazzled the crowd, but the other Aardvarks had played like they had never done before.

The rest of the season was a continuation of that first game. The Aardvarks won every game, and none of them were even close. Dot and Dash broke every school baseball record, and in the championship tournament, the Aardvarks swept the trophy. To Coach McNally, the whole season, and especially the tournament, was like a dream.

That summer, the Morse family moved away, and not much more was heard of Dot and Dash. Every once in a while, someone would see their names in the newspaper, including a clipping from Japan, where they had led a team from a U.S. Army base to the national championship.

As for the rest of the Aardvarks, something had changed forever. Although they never again had a perfect season, they were always in contention. The Aardvarks still loved the game as much as ever, their grades never slipped, and they still needed girls and boys to field a squad. That championship season had made a difference in the Aardvarks, however, and whenever they walked onto a baseball field, they felt they had a good chance to win the game.

GO

23 **The author says that the twins poke fun at themselves to show that —**

    A Coach McNally believes his team can win the championship this year.

    B even though the twins are good, other players contribute to the team.

    C a sense of humor is important to playing baseball.

    D they don't think they are better than other people.

24 **Based on what you read in the passage, which pair of words fits in this sentence?**

The Morse twins _____ the Aardvarks and _____ the team's confidence.

    F influenced...improved

    G joined...absorbed

    H left...diminished

    J abandoned...devastated

25 **Which of these explains why Coach McNally downplayed his squad's ability?**

    A He knew the Morse twins would leave the team after this season.

    B He had no confidence the team would do well during the season.

    C He wanted to surprise the other teams with the Aardvark's improved abilities.

    D He liked the team better when they always lost their games.

26 **Which of these best describes what happens in the passage?**

    F A school's baseball team has a history of enjoying the game but not playing well.

    G Two outstanding players improve a baseball team that is usually a loser.

    H A school baseball coach gets the championship team he always dreamed about.

    J The team that is usually a powerhouse loses a season opener to a far worse team.

GO

For numbers 27 through 30, choose the best answer to the question.

27 Which of these sentences states a fact?

   A Most people change jobs several times during their lives.

   B The best job you will ever have is your first job.

   C The most important thing a job provides is the friendship of your co-workers.

   D Rich people do easier work than poor people.

28 Benjamin is writing a story about his family's history. Which of these is most likely to be found in the middle of the story?

   F Today, the family is spread all over the the United States, but most of us live in the Northeast.

   G Although Spain had long been their home, several members of the family decided to come to the United States around the time of the Civil War.

   H Our family name can be easily traced back for hundreds of years because the majority of the family lived in the same region of Spain.

   J Because of a scrapbook my grandmother has been keeping, future generations will be able to look upon our past.

29 Which of these is most likely taken from a legend?

   A The caves were formed by water actually dissolving the rocks over many thousands of years.

   B No one has ever found the treasure, but the locals insist it is somewhere deep inside the cave.

   C The first settlers in the area, Native Americans, discovered the caves.

   D I can remember the first time my family visited the caves.

30 His guilt was a heavy burden he would bear throughout his life.

   What does this statement really mean?

   F He was guilty of stealing something valuable.

   G Feeling guilty made him eat a lot.

   H His strength allowed him to carry out crimes.

   J Being guilty was something he thought about often and it bothered him.

Example

Directions: Read the selection then mark the answer you think is correct.

E1

Alexandra looked at the mess in the kitchen. Someone had gotten into the trash and there was stuff all over the floor. It looked as if a tornado had hit the kitchen. It didn't take her long to figure out who the culprit was. Her dog, Barfley, was huddled up under the dining room table. His chin was on the floor and he had a guilty expression on his face.

A What do you think will happen next?

A Barfley will sniff the trash.

B Alexandra will walk the dog.

C Barfley will run away.

D Alexandra will scold Barfley.

Here is a passage about the part of the universe in which we live. Read the passage and then do numbers 1 through 8 on page 141.

The earth and the other planets in our solar system belong to a spiral galaxy called the Milky Way. The Milky Way is shaped like a disk with "arms" reaching out from a well defined center. Our solar system is far from the center of the galaxy, near the end of one of the arms. In galactic terms, we are way out in the boondocks.

Our solar system is not, however, at the edge of the galaxy. The corona or outermost formation in the Milky Way is at least 200,000 light-years from the center. Since a light-year, the distance traveled by light in one year, is about 5.9 trillion miles, the distance from one side of our galaxy to the other is almost unimaginable!

The stars in the galaxy, and there are many millions of them, are divided into two classifications, Population I and Population II. Population I stars, which are found in the arms of the spiral, contain elements heavier than helium and range in age from a few hundred thousand years to over ten billion years. Our sun is a Population I star.

Population II stars are all approximately 12 to 15 billion years old. They are located near the center of the galaxy and are composed of relatively light elements.

Until about fifty years ago, scientists thought our galaxy was the entire universe. Today, we know that our galaxy is just a small part of it, and that there are millions of other galaxies in the universe.

Trying to map our galaxy is not an easy task. In addition to dealing with millions of stars and huge distances, astronomers must try to "see" through galactic dust. The problem they face is much like the problem you would face looking out a very dirty window and trying to figure out who was walking up the road a mile away.

Scientists solved the problem by measuring the radio waves emitted by the stars. Radio waves pass through the dust and can be measured more accurately than light. Radio astronomy, as this technique is known, allowed scientists to paint a much more precise picture of our galaxy. They found that in addition to solar systems and dust clouds, our galaxy includes a black hole. This structure appears to be a collapsed star that is so dense that it actually absorbs light and attracts anything that comes near it. If an asteroid or a space ship got too close to a black hole, it would disappear into a *void* about which scientists know nothing.

GO ›

1   **According to this passage —**

   A Population II stars are generally older than Population I stars.

   B Population I stars are generally older than Population II stars.

   C Population I stars are generally larger than Population II stars.

   D Population II stars are generally larger than Population I stars.

2   **The author probably wrote this passage —**

   F to describe our solar system.

   G to explain what a light-year is.

   H to describe what a black hole is.

   J to explain the structure of the galaxy.

3   **What does the phrase "out in the boondocks" mean in this passage?**

   A Near the center of things

   B Far from the center of things

   C Poor

   D Small

4   **From this passage, you can conclude that —**

   F the galaxy and the universe are the same.

   G the number of stars can be counted exactly using radio waves.

   H distances in space are unimaginable.

   J spatial measurements are precise.

5   **A "void" in this passage is —**

   A a very heavy star.

   B an unknown region.

   C a spiral galaxy.

   D an asteroid.

6   **The author compares galactic dust to —**

   F fine particles.

   G unimaginable distances.

   H a dirty window.

   J radio waves.

7   **Because of the great distances involved in studying space, scientists —**

   A have a hard time seeing stars through telescopes.

   B can't use radio waves to study the stars through galactic dust.

   C know exactly what a black hole is and what causes them.

   D have a hard time actually proving their ideas are right or wrong.

8   **The earth is —**

   F part of the solar system and the galaxy.

   G part of the solar system but not the galaxy.

   H part of the galaxy but not the solar system.

   J part of neither the galaxy nor the solar system.

GO

In this story, a girl and her grandmother make an interesting discovery in the attic on a rainy day. Read the story, then do numbers 9 through 17.

Letters from the Past

It was a cold, rainy afternoon. Mary Lou and her grandmother were in the attic of her grandmother's Iowa farmhouse, entertaining themselves by looking through the contents of a battered, old trunk.

"These old clothes are a riot, Grandma. Did people really wear things like this?" asked Mary Lou smiling.

"They certainly did," replied Grandma. "Your aunts and uncles wore them and thought themselves elegant, indeed."

Mary Lou laughed and pulled an old candy box out of the trunk. She lifted the lid and found a packet of letters tied with string. "These letters look really old, Grandma. See how the envelopes are tattered and yellowed?"

"Look at the stamps, Mary Lou. You couldn't mail a letter today with a one cent stamp on it."

"Who wrote them?" asked Mary Lou, trying to read the flowing, graceful handwriting.

"Well, they are addressed to my mother and father, and the postmark shows they were mailed from Neversink, New York," Grandma noted as she flipped through the envelopes in the packet. "They are all from my father's mother whose name was Anna Thomas. I had forgotten all about them." Grandma removed the string from around the letters. She carefully opened an envelope and removed the letter.

"The writing is very fancy," commented Mary Lou as she stared at the letter.

"Telephones weren't available in Iowa until after 1900. If Anna Thomas wanted to stay in touch with her son and his wife who had moved from New York to Iowa, she had to do so by writing letters. Penmanship was very important, and people took pride in showing a fine hand," said Grandma.

"What does the letter say?" asked Mary Lou. Grandma adjusted her eyeglasses and read:

Dear Children,
I think you must have had a hard time building your house. When I read the newspapers and they told about the snowstorms, I could not sleep nights to think how hard you must have it. Jeanie, I was glad you sent me a lock of your hair. I will send you a lock of mine and wish you would send a lock of Arthur's. I will send you some of my lettuce seed. It is the headed kind. We all call it very good. Take it and cut it fine, put sugar and cream on it. You must have the plants about a foot apart and hoe it like you would cabbage. Write soon and have faith. There is trouble everywhere, and you will overcome yours.
Your loving mother, Anna

When Grandma finished reading, Mary Lou was quiet for a moment and then whispered, "I think she must have missed them a lot and worried about them because they were so far away from her."

"Yes, I'm sure she did. Anna never saw her children again, you know. The trip to Iowa was too much for her, and the children couldn't afford to leave the farm. But she wrote them almost every week, and they wrote back to her. Even though they were more than a thousand miles apart, they remained very close." Grandma looked at Mary Lou and put her arm around her. "We are fortunate to have these letters, Mary Lou. Someday when you have children, I hope you will read the letters to them. Nothing would please me more than to know my grandchildren had the opportunity to learn all about my grandmother's life."

GO

9 What made Mary Lou think the letters were old?

A They were in the trunk.

B The stamps were strange.

C They had pictures with them.

D They looked old and yellowed.

10 The postmark on an envelope shows —

F where the letter was mailed.

G who wrote the letter.

H where the letter is going.

J who will receive the letter.

11 Why were grandmother and Mary Lou going through the trunk?

A They like the attic.

B The electricity was out.

C There was not much else to do.

D It was too hot outside.

12 In this story, "showing a fine hand" means —

F having good penmanship.

G having nice hands.

H dressing with nice gloves.

J writing often to friends.

13 What surprised Mary Lou?

A Where the letters came from

B The way people dressed long ago

C That her grandmother wanted to go to the attic with her

D That people wrote to each other rather than using the telephone

14 Who wrote the letters Mary Lou found in the old trunk?

F Mary Lou's mother

G The mother and father of Grandma

H The mother of Grandma's father

J Mary Lou's grandmother

15 What does the word "elegant" mean in the third paragraph?

A Very unusual

B Funny

C Without many colors

D Showing good taste

16 In the letter Anna Thomas wrote to her family in Iowa, she said she could not sleep nights because —

F she had read about the snowstorm in the newspaper.

G she wanted a lock of her son's hair.

H she wanted Jeanie to grow lettuce from the seeds she sent.

J there was trouble everywhere.

17 At the end of the story, Grandma expresses her belief that —

A Mary Lou should write letters to her very often.

B she missed her children who lived far away.

C children should learn about their family's history.

D letters are the best way to learn about family members.

GO

Can something that tastes so delicious be good for you?

America has given the world many foods, one of which is the pecan. This tasty nut is a wonderful snack plain or roasted, and it adds flavor and crunch to all sorts of dishes. Moreover, pecans are healthful as well as delicious. They are a good source of protein and contain iron, calcium, potassium, phosphorous, magnesium, and B vitamins. They are also high in fiber and unsaturated fat. Unfortunately, pecans are also high in calories—190 calories per ounce—and that makes them fattening if eaten in great quantity.

People in the South have enjoyed finding and eating native pecans for centuries. The earliest French and Spanish explorers found that pecans were a staple part of the Native American diet. In fact, the name pecan comes from an Algonquin word that means "good to eat but with a hard shell." The trees naturally grow along riverbanks in the South. The rushing water carries nuts and deposits them in other places where they can sprout and grow. The warm climate in the South is perfect for pecan trees.

Native pecans are tasty and abundant, but the shells are very hard. Horticulturists have developed more than a thousand different varieties of pecans with thinner shells, called paper shell pecans. All of these varieties are *grafts*, which means a branch from a paper shell tree is attached to a cut made in the trunk of a young native tree. If it grows (or grafts), the other limbs of the native tree are cut off and only the paper shell limb develops. The root system is native, but the limbs and fruit are paper shell. This grafting process is necessary because only nuts from native trees, not paper shell pecan trees, can be planted to produce a new tree.

Most pecans are grown on farms today. The pecan tree farmer has to learn patience because a pecan tree must be six years old before it will bear fruit. A productive pecan farm can produce a thousand pounds of pecans per acre of trees. Georgia produces more of the country's commercial pecan crop than any other state, 46 percent. Texas is second with 26 percent.

Although pecans can be bought in stores year-round, many people plant paper shell pecan trees so they can grow their own nuts. The trees are attractive around a house, provide shade, and produce tasty nuts. In the American South, gathering native pecans is still a favorite fall activity. Families head out to the woods on a sunny afternoon with a picnic basket and a burlap sack. They enjoy their lunch and come home with a sack filled with delicious pecans.

GO >

18 Why must pecan farmers be patient?

F If you plant a pecan tree in spring, you won't get nuts until autumn.

G It takes a long time before a pecan tree grows nuts.

H It takes a long time to open a pecan shell because it is hard.

J Picking up pecans from the ground takes a long time.

19 In this passage, the term "graft" refers to —

A taking money illegally.

B something you do that requires a lot of talent.

C planting pecan trees.

D growing a limb from one tree on another tree.

20 What would grow if you planted a pecan from a paper shell tree?

F It would not grow.

G It would grow a native tree.

H It would grow roots from a native tree.

J It would take years to produce nuts.

21 In this passage, what tone does the author use?

A Uncertain

B Calming

C Factual

D Excited

22 In this passage, a "native tree" is one that —

F was planted by Native Americans.

G was grafted.

H has thin-shelled nuts.

J grows naturally.

23 This passage suggests that —

A pecan farmers make more money than other farmers.

B the pecan is the most healthful nut.

C pecan shells are tasty.

D pecans should be eaten in small quantities.

24 Pecan trees seem to grow best —

F where the weather is cold.

G where the weather is warm.

H in hot, dry ground.

J where the wind seems to blow often.

GO

Dragon's Tears

The folklore of China is filled with stories of dragons. In the ancient Chinese stories, dragons are not bad, and young men do not set out on quests to destroy them. Dragon emperors have beautiful daughters who want to find good, kind peasant husbands and live happily ever after on earth. One dragon story takes place in the province of Sichuan, which has twenty-four small lakes called Dragon's Tears. The story of their name is a favorite Chinese legend.

Wen Peng was a good, peasant boy who lived with his widowed mother. He fished and sold his catch to support himself and his mother. One day, he felt an enormous tug on his line. He fought and struggled and finally landed a huge, golden fish. The fish gasped, "Please, let me go, and I will reward you." Wen Peng felt sorry for the creature and returned it to the water. In return, the fish gave him a magic pearl.

With the magic pearl, Wen Peng and his mother had all they needed and were very happy. A jealous neighbor saw their prosperity and became very suspicious. "You are sending your son out to steal," he told Wen Peng's mother. "There is no other way for you to be doing so well." The mother was so frightened that she told the neighbor about the pearl.

This only increased the neighbor's jealousy, and he was determined to get the magic pearl. As soon as Wen Peng came into the house, he and his men grabbed the boy and began to shake him, demanding the pearl. Wen Peng had hidden the pearl in his mouth, and the shaking made him swallow it.

Wen Peng fainted, and when he woke, he asked his mother for water. He drank and drank but could not satisfy his thirst. He finally went down to the river where he had caught the fish. It seemed as if he would drink the river dry.

As darkness came, a huge storm arose. Wen Peng's mother watched in horror as her son slowly turned into a great dragon and started to fly away. She begged him not to go, but a gust of wind carried him into the sky as he called, "I am sorry, Mother. I cannot stay."

"Come back. Come back, my son," she continued to call. The dragon turned sadly, and great tears fell from his fiery eyes. After these drops fell to the ground, they formed the two dozen lakes of Sichuan.

GO

25 **Wen Peng can best be described as —**

A reasonable.

B responsible.

C greedy.

D jealous.

26 **Wen Peng let the golden fish go because —**

F the fish gave him a pearl.

G he felt sorry for the fish.

H he could not eat it.

J the neighbor came by.

27 **Another good title for this story is —**

A "The Boy and the Magic Pearl."

B "A Good Son."

C "Don't Go, My Son."

D "The Boy Who Became A Dragon."

28 **This story is a legend about —**

F a boy learning a lesson.

G why sons should love their mothers.

H the problems caused by greed.

J how twenty-four lakes were formed.

29 **There is enough information in this story to show that —**

A it could not really happen.

B people in China think dragons are real.

C Wen Peng was a bad son.

D thunder is caused by dragons.

30 **The jealous neighbor was determined to have —**

F all the family's money.

G the magic pearl.

H the power to turn into a dragon.

J the golden fish.

31 **In order to answer number 30, the best thing to do is —**

A skim the whole story several times.

B look at the beginning of each paragraph.

C look for the key word "neighbor."

D read the last paragraph.

GO

For numbers 32 through 35, choose the best answer to the question.

32 Which of these statements makes use of a metaphor?

F The snow was a blanket, covering the garden and burying the flowers that had just emerged from the ground.

G The whale seemed huge, bigger than any animal Vangie had ever seen, bigger even than her house.

H The brook made beautiful sounds, babbling over rocks and murmuring through undercut banks.

J The hawk soared over the field, circling slowly while it watched for any movement below.

33 The river port was locked in winter's harsh grip for months.

What does this description really mean?

A The port was locked up by the authorities.

B The winter was colder than usual near the river.

C Workers in the port were unfriendly in the winter.

D The river was frozen and the port was closed.

34 Dorothea Lange was chosen by the Farm Security Administration to record the migration of people from the Great Plains to California. Her photographs were so stunning that she was recognized as one of America's foremost photographers.

This passage would most likely be found in —

F an encyclopedia entry about migrations.

G a biography.

H a legend.

J a traveler's guide to the Great Plains.

35 Which of these descriptions of an airplane trip states a fact?

A The meal on the plane wasn't very tasty.

B Our cabin attendant certainly seemed pleasant.

C The plane took off almost an hour late.

D The ride was bumpier than I expected.

STOP

Grade 6 Answer Key

Page 106
- **A.** D
- **B.** F
- **1.** C
- **2.** J
- **3.** A
- **4.** F
- **5.** A
- **6.** H
- **7.** D
- **8.** G

Page 107
- **A.** C
- **B.** J
- **1.** B
- **2.** F
- **3.** D
- **4.** G
- **5.** D
- **6.** F
- **7.** C

Page 108
- **A.** C
- **B.** G
- **1.** C
- **2.** F
- **3.** D
- **4.** G
- **5.** B
- **6.** H
- **7.** A
- **8.** J

Page 109
- **A.** C
- **B.** G
- **1.** D
- **2.** F
- **3.** A
- **4.** J
- **5.** D

Page 110
- **A.** A
- **B.** J
- **1.** C
- **2.** G
- **3.** D
- **4.** F
- **5.** D
- **6.** G

Page 111
- **A.** C
- **B.** G
- **1.** D
- **2.** H
- **3.** A
- **4.** H
- **5.** B
- **6.** F

Page 112
- **E1.** D
- **E2.** F
- **1.** C
- **2.** F
- **3.** D
- **4.** H
- **5.** D
- **6.** G
- **7.** A
- **8.** H

Page 113
- **9.** D
- **10.** F
- **11.** B
- **12.** H
- **13.** D
- **14.** J
- **15.** C
- **16.** G
- **17.** D
- **18.** F
- **19.** A

Grade 6 Answer Key

Page 114
20. H
21. B
22. F
23. C
24. F
25. C
26. H
27. A

Page 115
28. H
29. A
30. G
31. D
32. J
33. C
34. F
35. B

Page 116
E1. C
E2. J
1. B
2. J
3. D
4. G
5. D
6. H
7. G
8. D

Page 117
9. D
10. F
11. B
12. J
13. C
14. F
15. B
16. F
17. D
18. H
19. B

Page 118
20. H
21. B
22. F
23. D
24. G
25. B
26. J
27. C

Page 119
28. G
29. A
30. H
31. A
32. F
33. B
34. J
35. C

Page 120
A. D
1. C
2. F
3. D
4. G

Page 121
A. A

Page 122
1. D
2. H
3. C
4. F
5. B
6. J
7. B
8. H

Grade 6 Answer Key

Page 124
  9. D
  10. H
  11. A
  12. G
  13. B
  14. H
  15. A
  16. J

Page 125
  A. C

Page 126
  1. A
  2. F
  3. D
  4. H
  5. D
  6. F
  7. B

Page 128
  8. H
  9. A
  10. J
  11. C
  12. F
  13. C
  14. F
  15. B

Page 130
  16. G
  17. D
  18. F
  19. C
  20. J
  21. B

Page 131
  A. B

Page 132
  1. D
  2. G
  3. C
  4. F
  5. A
  6. H

Page 134
  7. B
  8. H
  9. D
  10. J
  11. A
  12. H
  13. B
  14. F

Page 136
  15. A
  16. J
  17. C
  18. G
  19. A
  20. J
  21. D
  22. J

Page 138
  23. D
  24. F
  25. C
  26. G

Page 139
27. A
28. G
29. B
30. J

Page 140
A. D

Page 141
1. A
2. J
3. B
4. H
5. B
6. H
7. D
8. F

Page 143
9. D
10. F
11. C
12. F
13. B
14. H
15. D
16. F
17. C

Page 145
18. G
19. D
20. F
21. C
22. J
23. D
24. G

Page 147
25. B
26. G
27. D
28. J
29. A
30. G
31. C

Page 148
32. F
33. D
34. G
35. C

Fill in only one letter for each item. If you change an answer, make sure to erase your first mark completely.

Page 106

A. Ⓐ Ⓑ Ⓒ Ⓓ

B. Ⓕ Ⓖ Ⓗ Ⓙ

1. Ⓐ Ⓑ Ⓒ Ⓓ

2. Ⓕ Ⓖ Ⓗ Ⓙ

3. Ⓐ Ⓑ Ⓒ Ⓓ

4. Ⓕ Ⓖ Ⓗ Ⓙ

5. Ⓐ Ⓑ Ⓒ Ⓓ

6. Ⓕ Ⓖ Ⓗ Ⓙ

7. Ⓐ Ⓑ Ⓒ Ⓓ

8. Ⓕ Ⓖ Ⓗ Ⓙ

Page 107

A. Ⓐ Ⓑ Ⓒ Ⓓ

B. Ⓕ Ⓖ Ⓗ Ⓙ

1. Ⓐ Ⓑ Ⓒ Ⓓ

2. Ⓕ Ⓖ Ⓗ Ⓙ

3. Ⓐ Ⓑ Ⓒ Ⓓ

4. Ⓕ Ⓖ Ⓗ Ⓙ

5. Ⓐ Ⓑ Ⓒ Ⓓ

6. Ⓕ Ⓖ Ⓗ Ⓙ

7. Ⓐ Ⓑ Ⓒ Ⓓ

Page 108

A. Ⓐ Ⓑ Ⓒ Ⓓ

B. Ⓕ Ⓖ Ⓗ Ⓙ

1. Ⓐ Ⓑ Ⓒ Ⓓ

2. Ⓕ Ⓖ Ⓗ Ⓙ

3. Ⓐ Ⓑ Ⓒ Ⓓ

4. Ⓕ Ⓖ Ⓗ Ⓙ

5. Ⓐ Ⓑ Ⓒ Ⓓ

6. Ⓕ Ⓖ Ⓗ Ⓙ

7. Ⓐ Ⓑ Ⓒ Ⓓ

8. Ⓕ Ⓖ Ⓗ Ⓙ

Page 109

A. Ⓐ Ⓑ Ⓒ Ⓓ

B. Ⓕ Ⓖ Ⓗ Ⓙ

1. Ⓐ Ⓑ Ⓒ Ⓓ

2. Ⓕ Ⓖ Ⓗ Ⓙ

3. Ⓐ Ⓑ Ⓒ Ⓓ

4. Ⓕ Ⓖ Ⓗ Ⓙ

5. Ⓐ Ⓑ Ⓒ Ⓓ

Page 110

A. Ⓐ Ⓑ Ⓒ Ⓓ

B. Ⓕ Ⓖ Ⓗ Ⓙ

1. Ⓐ Ⓑ Ⓒ Ⓓ

2. Ⓕ Ⓖ Ⓗ Ⓙ

3. Ⓐ Ⓑ Ⓒ Ⓓ

4. Ⓕ Ⓖ Ⓗ Ⓙ

5. Ⓐ Ⓑ Ⓒ Ⓓ

6. Ⓕ Ⓖ Ⓗ Ⓙ

Page 111

A. Ⓐ Ⓑ Ⓒ Ⓓ

B. Ⓕ Ⓖ Ⓗ Ⓙ

1. Ⓐ Ⓑ Ⓒ Ⓓ

2. Ⓕ Ⓖ Ⓗ Ⓙ

3. Ⓐ Ⓑ Ⓒ Ⓓ

4. Ⓕ Ⓖ Ⓗ Ⓙ

5. Ⓐ Ⓑ Ⓒ Ⓓ

6. Ⓕ Ⓖ Ⓗ Ⓙ

Page 112

E1. Ⓐ Ⓑ Ⓒ Ⓓ

E2. Ⓕ Ⓖ Ⓗ Ⓙ

1. Ⓐ Ⓑ Ⓒ Ⓓ

2. Ⓕ Ⓖ Ⓗ Ⓙ

3. Ⓐ Ⓑ Ⓒ Ⓓ

4. Ⓕ Ⓖ Ⓗ Ⓙ

5. Ⓐ Ⓑ Ⓒ Ⓓ

6. Ⓕ Ⓖ Ⓗ Ⓙ

7. Ⓐ Ⓑ Ⓒ Ⓓ

8. Ⓕ Ⓖ Ⓗ Ⓙ

Page 113

9. Ⓐ Ⓑ Ⓒ Ⓓ

10. Ⓕ Ⓖ Ⓗ Ⓙ

11. Ⓐ Ⓑ Ⓒ Ⓓ

12. Ⓕ Ⓖ Ⓗ Ⓙ

13. Ⓐ Ⓑ Ⓒ Ⓓ

14. Ⓕ Ⓖ Ⓗ Ⓙ

15. Ⓐ Ⓑ Ⓒ Ⓓ

16. Ⓕ Ⓖ Ⓗ Ⓙ

17. Ⓐ Ⓑ Ⓒ Ⓓ

18. Ⓕ Ⓖ Ⓗ Ⓙ

19. Ⓐ Ⓑ Ⓒ Ⓓ

Page 114

20. Ⓕ Ⓖ Ⓗ Ⓙ

21. Ⓐ Ⓑ Ⓒ Ⓓ

22. Ⓕ Ⓖ Ⓗ Ⓙ

23. Ⓐ Ⓑ Ⓒ Ⓓ

24. Ⓕ Ⓖ Ⓗ Ⓙ

25. Ⓐ Ⓑ Ⓒ Ⓓ

26. Ⓕ Ⓖ Ⓗ Ⓙ

27. Ⓐ Ⓑ Ⓒ Ⓓ

Page 115

28. Ⓕ Ⓖ Ⓗ Ⓙ

29. Ⓐ Ⓑ Ⓒ Ⓓ

30. Ⓕ Ⓖ Ⓗ Ⓙ

31. Ⓐ Ⓑ Ⓒ Ⓓ

32. Ⓕ Ⓖ Ⓗ Ⓙ

33. Ⓐ Ⓑ Ⓒ Ⓓ

34. Ⓕ Ⓖ Ⓗ Ⓙ

35. Ⓐ Ⓑ Ⓒ Ⓓ

Page 116

E1. Ⓐ Ⓑ Ⓒ Ⓓ

E2. Ⓕ Ⓖ Ⓗ Ⓙ

1. Ⓐ Ⓑ Ⓒ Ⓓ

2. Ⓕ Ⓖ Ⓗ Ⓙ

3. Ⓐ Ⓑ Ⓒ Ⓓ

4. Ⓕ Ⓖ Ⓗ Ⓙ

5. Ⓐ Ⓑ Ⓒ Ⓓ

6. Ⓕ Ⓖ Ⓗ Ⓙ

7. Ⓐ Ⓑ Ⓒ Ⓓ

8. Ⓕ Ⓖ Ⓗ Ⓙ

Page 117

9. Ⓐ Ⓑ Ⓒ Ⓓ

10. Ⓕ Ⓖ Ⓗ Ⓙ

11. Ⓐ Ⓑ Ⓒ Ⓓ

12. Ⓕ Ⓖ Ⓗ Ⓙ

13. Ⓐ Ⓑ Ⓒ Ⓓ

14. Ⓕ Ⓖ Ⓗ Ⓙ

15. Ⓐ Ⓑ Ⓒ Ⓓ

16. Ⓕ Ⓖ Ⓗ Ⓙ

17. Ⓐ Ⓑ Ⓒ Ⓓ

18. Ⓕ Ⓖ Ⓗ Ⓙ

19. Ⓐ Ⓑ Ⓒ Ⓓ

Page 118

20. Ⓕ Ⓖ Ⓗ Ⓙ

21. Ⓐ Ⓑ Ⓒ Ⓓ

22. Ⓕ Ⓖ Ⓗ Ⓙ

23. Ⓐ Ⓑ Ⓒ Ⓓ

24. Ⓕ Ⓖ Ⓗ Ⓙ

29. (A) (B) (C) (D)

26. (F) (G) (H) (J)

27. (A) (B) (C) (D)

Page 119

28. (F) (G) (H) (J)

29. (A) (B) (C) (D)

30. (F) (G) (H) (J)

31. (A) (B) (C) (D)

32. (F) (G) (H) (J)

33. (A) (B) (C) (D)

34. (F) (G) (H) (J)

35. (A) (B) (C) (D)

Page 120

A. (A) (B) (C) (D)

1. (A) (B) (C) (D)

2. (F) (G) (H) (J)

3. (A) (B) (C) (D)

4. (F) (G) (H) (J)

Page 121

A. (A) (B) (C) (D)

Page 122

1. (A) (B) (C) (D)

2. (F) (G) (H) (J)

3. (A) (B) (C) (D)

4. (F) (G) (H) (J)

5. (A) (B) (C) (D)

6. (F) (G) (H) (J)

7. (A) (B) (C) (D)

8. (F) (G) (H) (J)

Page 124

9. (A) (B) (C) (D)

10. (F) (G) (H) (J)

11. (A) (B) (C) (D)

12. (F) (G) (H) (J)

13. (A) (B) (C) (D)

14. (F) (G) (H) (J)

15. (A) (B) (C) (D)

16. (F) (G) (H) (J)

Page 125

A. (A) (B) (C) (D)

Page 126

1. (A) (B) (C) (D)

2. (F) (G) (H) (J)

3. (A) (B) (C) (D)

4. (F) (G) (H) (J)

5. (A) (B) (C) (D)

6. (F) (G) (H) (J)

7. (A) (B) (C) (D)

Page 128

8. (F) (G) (H) (J)

9. (A) (B) (C) (D)

10. (F) (G) (H) (J)

11. (A) (B) (C) (D)

12. (F) (G) (H) (J)

13. (A) (B) (C) (D)

14. (F) (G) (H) (J)

15. (A) (B) (C) (D)

Page 130

16. (F) (G) (H) (J)

17. (A) (B) (C) (D)

18. (F) (G) (H) (J)

19. (A) (B) (C) (D)

20. (F) (G) (H) (J)

21. (A) (B) (C) (D)

Page 131

A. (A) (B) (C) (D)

Page 132

1. (A) (B) (C) (D)

2. (F) (G) (H) (J)

3. (A) (B) (C) (D)

4. (F) (G) (H) (J)

5. (A) (B) (C) (D)

6. (F) (G) (H) (J)

Page 134

7. (A) (B) (C) (D)

8. (F) (G) (H) (J)

9. (A) (B) (C) (D)

10. (F) (G) (H) (J)

11. (A) (B) (C) (D)

12. (F) (G) (H) (J)

13. (A) (B) (C) (D)

14. (F) (G) (H) (J)

Page 136

15. (A) (B) (C) (D)

16. (F) (G) (H) (J)

17. (A) (B) (C) (D)

18. (F) (G) (H) (J)

19. (A) (B) (C) (D)

20. (F) (G) (H) (J)

21. (A) (B) (C) (D)

22. (F) (G) (H) (J)

Page 138

23. (A) (B) (C) (D)

24. (F) (G) (H) (J)

25. (A) (B) (C) (D)

26. (F) (G) (H) (J)

Page 139

27. (A) (B) (C) (D)

28. (F) (G) (H) (J)

29. (A) (B) (C) (D)

30. (F) (G) (H) (J)

Page 140

A. (A) (B) (C) (D)

Page 141

1. (A) (B) (C) (D)

2. (F) (G) (H) (J)

3. (A) (B) (C) (D)

4. (F) (G) (H) (J)

5. (A) (B) (C) (D)

6. (F) (G) (H) (J)

7. (A) (B) (C) (D)

8. (F) (G) (H) (J)

Page 143

9. (A) (B) (C) (D)

10. (F) (G) (H) (J)

11. (A) (B) (C) (D)

12. (F) (G) (H) (J)

13. (A) (B) (C) (D)

14. (F) (G) (H) (J)

15. (A) (B) (C) (D)

16. (F) (G) (H) (J)

17. (A) (B) (C) (D)

Page 145

18. (F) (G) (H) (J)

19. (A) (B) (C) (D)

20. (F) (G) (H) (J)

21. (A) (B) (C) (D)

22. (F) (G) (H) (J)

23. (A) (B) (C) (D)

24. (F) (G) (H) (J)

Page 147

25. (F) (G) (H) (J)

26. (A) (B) (C) (D)

27. (F) (G) (H) (J)

28. (A) (B) (C) (D)

29. (F) (G) (H) (J)

30. (A) (B) (C) (D)

31. (F) (G) (H) (J)

Page 148

32. (F) (G) (H) (J)

33. (A) (B) (C) (D)

34. (F) (G) (H) (J)

35. (A) (B) (C) (D)